Girlfriends

Dr. Beverly M. Donovan

*Phenomenal Woman —
May God continue to
richly bless you —
Love Dr. Beverly Donovan*

Dedication

This labor of love is dedicated to my two beautiful daughters,
my beloved mother whom I will meet in Glory,
my two sisters,
all of my girlfriends,
the older women who have influenced who I am today,
and the younger ladies coming after me, blazing their own courses.

Girlfriends, If we never meet here, may we get to know each other over there.

Love,
Girlfriend Bev

The Girls

in particular order...

Grace

Mercy

Charity

Faith

Hope

Favor

Serenity

Honesty

Harmony

Patience

Prudence

Justice

Joy

Glory

You

Proverbial Portraits

Which Girlfriend are You Most Like?

The Parting Sentiment of Each Girlfriend's Heart

The Butterfly

Left wing (upper): ornate, fragile, tender, beautiful, intricate, colorful, industrious, elegant, persistent, graceful

Right wing (upper): soft, precious, gorgeous, amigable, amazing, sociable, shy, bold, quiet, winged, shapely, metamorphic

Left wing (lower): free, capable, unique, independent, delicate, detailed

Right wing (lower): adventurous, productive, cute, lovely, industrious, harmless

The Woman

Introduction

The Butterfly is known to be one of the most beautiful of God's creations. Though I believe it is impossible to accurately rank the beauty of God's many masterpieces; for the ocean, mountains, rivers, valleys, the sky, earth, stars, moon, sun, animals, and humans each boasts amazing beauty; the butterfly would make the list of many when asked. The butterfly symbolizes more than magnificent beauty to me when likened to women. The butterfly symbolizes a woman to me because of the metamorphosis it undergoes throughout its four life stages; that of an egg, the larva, pupa and an adult. Though direct correlations would not be made between the woman's and the butterfly's physical life cycles; I will make correlations between the metamorphosis that both a butterfly and a woman undergo in order to blossom.

Both woman and butterfly go through stages of confinement, restriction and resignation. They each wrestle through that stage and move on to the next, wherein they may experience loss, distress, struggle, feelings of insecurity, weight gain, and a search for who they will become. This temporary stage is one of the most daunting for it is during this stage that you can be physically seen, yet discounted; possess beauty and life, yet it not be recognized; struggle to and through the transformation, yet be misunderstood, forsaken, forgotten, degraded or discouraged.

In the next stage, to the eye, there is more ready evidence of the magnificence, the potential, the beauty, the wonder, the promise and potential of the butterfly. It is at this stage that both the butterfly and the woman can most appreciate the struggle they've been through. They can faintly see beyond the horizon what they may become, who they may be, who they were meant to be, who they influence, who they will touch, who will touch them, and who they are. The anticipative rest during this stage, allows time for reflection. It is during this stage that their life is taken into perspective, they assess what they've been through; and their wings begin to flutter in expectation of what they will become. The adult stage is the shortest life stage for a butterfly unless they hibernate during the winter months. Like a woman, their beauty is fleeting, their awe is short-lived and the struggle continues, as during the adult stage, a butterfly's sole purpose is to mate.

Whereas, the beautiful butterfly only goes through each stage once, physically, the human female may go through each cycle symbolically many times during her life. The stages for the human female are not physical, logical, or sequential, instead they are figurative representations of the time periods in her life, times when she may feel confined, and restricted; reflective and contemplative; and or be flamboyant, feeling beautiful and maternalistic and/or experience loss and depression.

Regardless of which stage, each reader may currently be in, it is important to note that life is cyclical. It is important to note, that God is aware of which stage you are currently experiencing and is both faithful and just, is kind and responsive, is supportive and life-changing. He listens to us, hears our hearts, sees our needs, and grants us some of our desires and all of our needs.

He has answered in His word, every one of our many questions about life, survival, support, help, hope, love, marriage, church, etc. He has provided us examples through the lives of men and women of the Bible some of great character, some unscrupulous, some of great wealth and some with the widow's mite, some with palace and princes, some paupers at the door of the temple, some with wisdom and valor, others with trickery and disgrace. He has before time began, penned a blueprint for us to follow. If we build our lives, our homes, our churches, our relationships, our very existence with the counsel in His word, our lives would be so much richer, and so much more in line with His plan for us.

I have become convinced that our God knew that at various times in a woman's life we would need to lean unashamed on the shoulders of another woman. He knew we would need to rely on the courage of Esther, the prudence of Abigail, the honesty and just character of Deborah, the hope of Sarah, the faith of Elisabeth, and the strength of Mary, His mother. He knew that the stories of these matriarchs of old would provide us answers to many of life's questions, and would inspire us to serve God as they did. I, in this manuscript, contend that He has, in His wisdom, provided us with fourteen other 'women' upon whom we can lean unashamed, depend on, call upon, and emulate. I refer to them affectionately as *The Girls*. Do allow me to introduce them to you.

This tribute to some of the least celebrated women of the Bible was birthed upon reflection primarily on the grace and mercy of God. I spent time thinking about how much the grace of God impacted my life; made me who I am, placed me where I am and granted me blessings beyond what I could ask for or knew I needed. Upon grateful reflection on what God has done for me, I could see evidences of His divine favor in my life. For my life was saturated with favor, for I was alive, had food and shelter and am blessed beyond what I deserve.

Though Grace, Mercy and Favor seemed to be ever present with me; I was keenly aware that there were other women with whom I were friends and who I needed to befriend. It became apparent to me that many other women were friends to me and made their presence known when I most needed them. They would show up unannounced, 'ring my phone', call my name, reach out to me, etc, just when I needed their virtue to be renewed in my life. Those, though they only visited for a while, and were seasonal visitors, proved to be friends for whom I was exceedingly grateful.

I asked my daughters to name other women in the Bible that fit the descriptions of women like Grace; that had personalities that were not explicitly described, had characteristics that were prominent but not often stated and whose impact in our lives was pronounced though overlooked or taken for granted. It was this reflection that allowed me the opportunity to name with my daughters' assistance these heroines of the Bible, these females that make such an impact on our lives, behind the scenes, and without whose friendships we would not be the girlfriends we are today. For they befriend you, give you comfort, make you feel worthy and love you unconditionally.

These fourteen powerful women inspire you to be better; to be great; to be phenomenal, to commit yourself spiritually, to love God, to trust God and to seek and walk in His will! Without their friendship, there is no way that you can navigate the wiles of this world, can meet the challenges this world presents you, can endure and sustain your promise, live your purpose or arrive at your desired end.

This candid introduction to these women of God is intended to equip you with their enduring attributes, inspire you, motivate you, keep you, bless you, bring you joy and peace, transform your thinking, your life, and have you to live your purpose and at long last, attain glory. In the next few pages, I excitedly introduce you, in candid descriptions, to the girlfriends; Grace, Mercy, Charity, Faith, Hope, Favor, Serenity, Honesty, Harmony, Patience, Prudence, Justice, Joy, Glory and yourself. This unique circle of friends will provide an impenetrable support system for you, will keep you grounded, lift you up in prayer, celebrate you in success, comfort you in grief, sustain you in trials and render you victorious.

I encourage you to know each of the girlfriends intimately; to learn and emulate their attributes as evidenced in their own lives as well as in the lives of the women named from them; to apply their counsel to your lives and to live every day as each of them would as their natural disposition has them so inclined.

Daily, take their parting sentiment to you to heart in love. Forever commit to it in hope. I implore you to walk in the everlasting peace that their heartfelt parting sentiment provides to you.

Girlfriend Grace

Gift of God

pReferential

Abundant

suffiCient

freE

Grace

Definition: the free and unmerited favor of God.

Origin: Latin

Meaning: Goodness and Generosity

Bible Verses:
Romans 5 v. 20
Moreover the law entered, that the offence might abound. But where sin abounded, grace did much more abound.

2 Corinthians 12:8-9
8 For this thing I besought the Lord thrice, that it might depart from me.
9 And he said unto me, My grace is sufficient for thee: for my strength is made perfect in weakness. Most gladly therefore will I rather glory in my infirmities, that the power of Christ may rest upon me.

Ephesians 2 v. 8-9
8 For by grace are ye saved through faith; and that not of yourselves: it is the gift of God:
9 Not of works, lest any man should boast.

Bible Reference: Grace was born in Genesis.
Genesis 3

In the book of Genesis, God created us out of love and redeemed us by Grace. He knew we were going to sin and disobey from as early as we were made, but yet He made us. He set forth a plan of redemption for us; an undeserved plan; an unmerited plan called Grace. We did not deserve it; for God was abundantly clear with his instructions to Adam and Eve, our foreparents, as to what He wanted them to do. When they disobeyed, God did not forsake His creation, instead He granted unto us, Grace.

Women of Grace in the Bible:
- *Anna* fasted and prayed day and night in spite of being married to a callous drunkard who did not appreciate her. *(1 Samuel 25:1-42; 2 Samuel 3:3)*

- *Dorcas* - earned fame and prestige for her dress-making. She was also an avid philanthropist and she gave away everything she had and could to those in need to the honor and glory of God. *(Acts 9:36-43)*
- Esther obtained grace and favor in the King's eyes instead of Queen Vashti. (The Book of Esther)
- *Hagar* - ill-treated by Sarah, her owner, she obeyed God's command to return to her. Upon her obedience, God made a promise that her son would be a father to a great multitude. (Genesis 16; 21:9-17; 25:12; Galatians 4:24, 25)
- *Hannah*, the favored wife of Elkanah could not bare children, suffered at the tongue of Elkanah's second wife and was after prayer and supplication granted grace and mercy in her son, Samuel. (1 Samuel 1; 2:1, 21)
- *Harlot mother, (there were two),* would rather live without her child than have him severed in two because of the untrue word of her callous companion spoken before King Solomon claiming the remaining living child was hers. (1 Kings 3)
- *Joanna*, having being shown grace and mercy by being healed from her infirmities, was numbered as one of Jesus' disciples and ministered to Jesus. (Luke 8: 1-3)
- *Jehosheba*, a princess married to a high priest, courageously stole her nephew Joash to preserve his life and the royal seed of the line of Judah. (2 Kings 11:2; 2 Chronicles 22:11)
- *Jochebed*, mother of Moses, devised a clever plan to have his life graciously spared so that he could become one of the greatest leaders to the people of Israel in the Bible. (Exodus 1; 2:1-11; 6:20; Numbers 26:59; Hebrews 11:23)
- *Leah*, Jacob's first wife, bore him six sons which were to be six of the twelve tribes of Israel. Though despised by her younger sister, Jacob's second wife, she remained faithful to her husband and to God. The naming of her first four sons testified of this as their names mean; Behold a son, Hearing, Joined, and Praise. (Genesis 29; 30; 49:31; Ruth 4:11)
- *Martha*, was gracious and hospitable to Jesus. (Luke 10:38-41; John 11; 12:1-3)
- *Mary*, for anointing Jesus' feet with her alabaster box of ointment. (Matthew 1; 2; 12:46; Luke 1; 2; John 2:1-11; 19:25; Acts 1:14)
- *Pharaoh's daughter*, the female savior of the people of Israel as she showed compassion and showered Moses with favor as her son in the palace of Pharaoh graciously allowing him a nurse who was his birth mother. (Exodus 2:5-10; Acts 7:21; Hebrews 11:24)
- *Rahab*, hid the men of God, and provided them a way to avoid sure death while placing herself on the treason punishable road herself. Instead of punishment, she was offered grace as God spared her and her family from Jericho's impending doom. (Joshua 2:1, 3; 6:17-25)

- Saul's sons by Milcah and *Rizpah* (7 in all) were hung in revenge for Saul breaking an oath he'd made with the Gibeonites. All seven bodies were guarded by Rizpah, mother of two of them, to disallow the bodies to be ravished by natural scavengers until the rain came, after which the bodies were buried. (2 Samuel 3:7; 21:8-14)
- *Salome*, wife of Zebedee, mother of James and John two of Jesus' disciples, showed grace and mercy to Jesus as she was one of the saintly women who followed and was hospitable to Jesus, witnessed his crucifixion and shared in the glorious news of his resurrection. (Matthew 20:20-24; 27:56; Mark 10:35-40; 15:40, 41; 16:1, 2)
- *Wench of En-Rogel,* thwarted Absalom's plan against his father by covering an empty well thereby hiding David's men. She also sent them in a direction away from David's men thereby dispensing grace to David and his men. (2 Samuel 17:17-19)
- *Widow of Zarephath,* though preparing for both her and her son's death after their last meal was prepared from what they had in store; she was able to sustain Elijah and her family during his sojourn with them and beyond as God multiplied her pantry holdings. (1 Kings 17:8-24; Luke 4:25, 26)
- *Widow in debt,* was able to sell the oil the Lord graciously blessed her with after all the borrowed vessels were filled. She was able to pay her debt and live comfortably thereafter. (2 Kings 4:1-7)
- *Woman of Shunem,* harmoniously and graciously provided her home and the apartment she built for him as a dwelling for Elisha as he traveled telling of Christ. In return for her gratitude, she received the promise of and later a son, making her a woman of joy. The son later died and Elisha at the request of his grief-stricken mother restored him to life. (2 Kings 4:8-37; 8:1-6)

About Grace:

Grace only has thoughts that are good and generous. She always wants to give to others, thinks about their needs and wants and then works to bring them to pass. Grace acts on those thoughts of good and generosity by doing good for others. She likes to spread goodness and make others happy by surprising them and giving them what they do not deserve. She likes giving gifts; her favorite being the free gift that only God could give. She specializes in planting seeds of kindness, prosperity and favor wherever she treads and to whomever she meets for no one deserves Grace, no one could work to earn her or lay claim to her without Faith.

Grace has feelings of only love and affection toward those she will befriend. Her emotions are always tender toward those she befriends for she is fond of them; she loves them. All who know Grace have only pleasant things to say about her; they appreciate her friendship and are positive that it is only because of their association with Grace that they themselves exist. Grace loves you and offers you unconditional love which she demonstrates daily by offering you God's favor. Grace is partial to you; she prefers you! She gives you special treatment! She chooses you! She rewards you though you could not possibly repay her or even appreciate her friendship enough.

Because of Grace:

Gratitude is a natural, logical and reflexive reaction to having experienced grace. Anyone, including the most detested, unworthy and unrepentant sinner is humbled and buckles into a posture of gratitude immediately after experiencing grace. There is no other posture that is acceptable after one experiences the unmerited favor of God. Grace is so undeserved, so unexpected, so overwhelming that angry feelings are pacified, hateful tongues are silenced, evil hearts are turned heavenward, all after being touched by grace. For Grace covers all that is not of God and transforms our thoughts, feelings and actions into a position of perpetual gratitude. We remain grateful for we may have been provided a glimpse of what we would have become were it not for Grace. We remain grateful for we are able to recognize upon reflection just how disgusting, distasteful and demoralizing our behavior had become. We remain grateful for we, because of Grace, are finally able to see what we can become, how our lives, our thoughts, our everything is transformed under the amazing and redeeming grace extended to us, though undeserved. Grace is a friend to you when you are in a perpetual posture of gratitude.

Being ***gracious*** to others is another sure sign of one's encounter with grace. Being gracious to others requires you to be selfless, self-sacrificing and self-denying. It requires the same qualities of the receiver of grace as it does the one who dispenses grace. In order to dispense grace, God himself, was selfless, self-sacrificing and self-denying. By giving us His Only Begotten Son he was selfless. He died at terrible death, thereby was self-sacrificing. He went on to live a life void of the recognition, love, and acceptance He rightfully deserved, rendering him self-denying. The dispensation of grace demands that you in turn dispense grace to others, that you selfishly deny yourself and sacrifice yourself for someone else's benefit.

An equally natural response to the receipt of grace is ***glorification***. Glorification is to give high praise, to exalt, to give glory especially through worship. Someone to whom grace is afforded, would be overflowing with gratitude, and would most appropriately evidence itself in exuberant glorification. Because of Grace, the receiver of grace will loudly declare the sentiment of Psalm 34 v. 1, "I will bless the Lord at all times; his praise shall continually be in my mouth. Someone who is experiencing a perpetual season of glorification, because of Grace, will never stop praising, never stop worshipping, never stop exalting God for ALL that he's done for them.

In earnest, this should be the sentiment of all of mankind, for we were all extended and are being extended grace. For certain, it should be the commitment of every born again believer, for it is by grace we have been saved, through faith. Our testimony as believers is glorification.

As a friend:

Grace is the girlfriend that takes our abuses, excuses our mistakes, loves us in spite of, is always there, shows up when we need her, the one we can't repay, the one we don't deserve.

She is loyal, insistent, supportive, compassionate, faithful, trustworthy, gracious, humble, loving and kind.

When Grace enters a room, she does not make a grand entrance, she does not need to be seen, recognized or acknowledged. She comes with a purpose, a plan, and a promise to grant you the unmerited favor of God. Grace visits unannounced; she does not call before she comes over, for she knows we don't know when we will need her, she is on-call, at our service, present whether we call or not, and costs us nothing.

When Grace gets together with you, she does not expect to take, her only intent is to give; give what we don't deserve, could not earn, can't buy nor truly appreciate. Grace is generous; she will go undone to be sure that her friend has what she needs and sometimes wants. She is the friend that never forgets your birthday, brings a gift to the party she threw for you and stay for clean up after all your other friends have gone on home. Grace is that friend to whom you may not have spoken to for a while, but yet she has 'followed you', kept up with your shenanigans; played a role in more of your life than you realized and befriended you despite how you show friendship to her.

Girlfriend to Girlfriend:

- My gifts from God to you are free and marked as yours.
- Receive, appreciate and give thanks for my gifts.
- Replicate my giving spirit; when blessed, bless someone else.
- Give selfishly of your time, energies, resources to someone else.
- Life and time are evidences of me; spend them wisely.

Grace in Quotation Marks:

"Grace is a generous gift of undeserved goodness."

Her Hashtags:

#free
#undeserved
#unmerited
#madblessings
#preferential
#abundant
#sufficient
#limitless
#giftofGod

Your Turn

_____
_____
_____

Recognizing Grace:
- Life
- Waking up
- Breathing
- Family
- House
- Car
- Mental stability
- Career
- Bills paid
- Shelter in life's storms
- Salvation
- Redemption
- Your very existence

Your Turn

- _____
- _____
- _____

Acknowledgement:

    I thank you God, for Grace. I know that Grace has been there for me since the beginning of time and is only granted by you. I need a friend in my life like Grace. Help me to recognize and appreciate Grace for who you created her to be. Help me to appreciate, love and glorify You from whom Grace receives her power.

Reflection on Grace

1. Your thoughts to or about Grace -

   _____
   _____
   _____
   _____
   _____
   _____
   _____

2. Which Biblical woman of grace do you most readily identify with and why?

   _____
   _____
   _____

3. Study the list of women of grace, what were their professions? What does this say about God's choices of women of grace?

Woman	Profession
What does this say about God's choices of women of grace?	

14

4. Ponder each of the Bible verses related to Grace. Which of the verses speak to you at your current need? How?

_____

_____

_____

_____

_____

_____

5. Recall and relate a recent time when you were granted or dispensed grace by or to someone else.

_____

_____

_____

_____

_____

_____

6. What might be Grace's advice to you about life in general?

_____

_____

_____

7. Write and then repeat your prayer to God concerning Grace.

_____

_____

_____
_____
_____
_____
_____
_____
_____

8. Having read about Grace, which christian songs or hymns could be her anthem? Make a list of them below. Listen to them and share them with someone else.

_____
_____
_____
_____
_____
_____
_____

9. As Grace goes with us everywhere; create a personalized license plate to help remind you about Grace.

Assignment:
1. Treat someone to lunch today.
2. Meet someone's need today.
3. Tip the waiter well after dinner.
4. Forgive someone for a wrong done to you.
5. Pray that someone would be granted grace because of your prayers.
6. Give someone the right of way in traffic.
7. Call up a girlfriend and tell them how much you appreciate them.
8. Visit a nursing home and read a book to someone.
9. Take care of yourself mentally; enjoy nature, sit by the beach or on your porch, look at the stars, get a massage, have your nails done, do your hair, etc.
10. Call or write to your child's teacher and encourage them in some way.

Girlfriend Mercy

coMpassionate

plEntiful

foRgiving

Caring

grants clemencY

Mercy

Definition: compassion or forgiveness shown toward someone

Origin: Latin

Meaning: Compassion

Bible Verses:
2 Samuel 24 v. 14
And David said unto Gad, I am in a great strait: let us fall now into the hand of the Lord; for his mercies are great: and let me not fall into the hand of man.

1 Peter 1 v. 3
Blessed be the God and Father of our Lord Jesus Christ, which according to his abundant mercy hath begotten us again unto a lively hope by the resurrection of Jesus Christ from the dead,

Hebrews 4 v. 16
Let us therefore come boldly unto the throne of grace, that we may obtain mercy, and find grace to help in time of need.

Bible Reference:
Genesis 3

Grace and Mercy are two siblings of a set of triplets! Consequently, Mercy was born in Genesis at the same time Grace was born. Mercy is the second eldest of the two by a second or so; for as God knows and knew everything before it happened, He knew that Adam and Eve were not going to be able to resist the temptation and to be obedient to His word. He, because of Charity, ensured that Grace and Mercy would befriend Adam and Eve and every one of their descendents.

Adam and Eve were extended mercy when God, despite their sin, did not vanquish them from the beautiful garden of Eden; nor take back the breath from their nostrils. He because of Mercy showed compassion and forgiveness to the disobedient pair.

Women of Mercy in the Bible:

- *Dorcas* - earned fame and prestige for her dress-making. She was also an avid philanthropist and she gave away everything she had and could to those in need and to the honor and glory of God. (Acts 9:36-43)
- *Hagar* - ill-treated by Sarah, Hagar was sent from the house of Abraham and Sarah. Just when she thought she and her son were going to die in the wilderness, she prayed to God and he granted her mercy and provided her a well from which to draw.
- *Hannah*, the favored wife of Elkanah could not bare children, suffered at the tongue of Elkanah's second wife and was, after prayer and supplication, granted mercy and was given Samuel.
- *Harlot mother, (there were two),* would rather live without her child than have him severed in two because of the untrue word of her callous companion spoken before King Solomon that claimed the remaining living child was hers. (1 Kings 3)
- *Jehosheba,* a princess married to a high priest, courageously stole her nephew Joash to preserve his life and the royal seed of the line of Judah. (2 Kings 11:2; 2 Chronicles 22:11)
- *Joanna*, having being shown grace and mercy by being healed from her infirmities, was numbered as one of Jesus' disciples and ministered to Jesus. (Luke 8 1-3)
- *Jochebed,* mother of Moses, devised a clever plan to have his life spared so that he could become one of the greatest leaders to the people of Israel in the Bible. Exodus 1; 2:1-11; 6:20; Numbers 26:59; Hebrews 11:23
- *Pharaoh's daughter*, the female savior of the people of Israel had mercy on the baby Moses by taking him to the palace allowing him a nurse who was his birth mother. (Exodus 2:5-10; Acts 7:21; Hebrews 11:24)
- *Rahab*, recognizing the dread evidenced by the visitors to her brothel that evening, and the understanding that she was being called out by God to serve them, hid the men of God, and provided them a way to avoid sure death while placing herself on the treason punishable road herself. (Joshua 2:1, 3; 6:17-25)
- Saul's sons by *Milcah and Rizpah* (7 in all) were hung in revenge for Saul breaking an oath he'd made with the Gibeonites. All seven bodies were guarded by Rizpah to disallow the bodies to be ravished by natural scavengers until the rain came, after which the bodies were buried. (2 Samuel 3:7; 21:8-14)

- *Wench of En-Rogel,* thwarted Absalom's plan against his father by covering an empty well thereby hiding David's men. She also sent them in a direction away from David's men which they pursued. (2 Samuel 17:17-19)
- *Widow of Zarephath,* though preparing for both her and her son's death after their last meal was prepared from what they had in store; she was able to sustain Elijah and her family during his sojourn with them and beyond as God mercifully multiplied her pantry holdings. (1 Kings 17:8-24)
- *Widow in debt,* was able to sell the oil the Lord mercifully blessed her with after all the borrowed vessels were filled. She was able to pay her debt and live comfortably thereafter. (2 Kings 4:1-7)
- *Woman of Shunem,* harmoniously and graciously provided her home and the apartment she built for Elisha as he traveled telling of Christ. In return for her gratitude, she received the promise of and later a son, making her a woman of joy. The son later died and Elisha at the request of his grief stricken mother restored the son to life. (2 Kings 4:8-37; 8:1-6)

About Mercy:

All are indebted to, appreciative of and in awe of Mercy. Mercy is asked for and requested incessantly especially when we are in a tight spot and the need for help or an emergency arises. Everyone is indebted to Mercy because they cannot repay her. Mercy does all that she does without any expectation of repayment. They are appreciative of Mercy because their lives would be different, providing they still had life, if it weren't for Mercy.

She stands in the gap, takes the punishment for, and spares the offender from the retaliation and consequences they deserve. They are in awe of Mercy, primarily because they cannot fathom how she forgives without question. Mercy has the uncanny ability and divine directive to absorb the hurts, ills and harm that she did not instigate, all without complaint or grudge.

Mercy looks for opportunities to bless people. Mercy stands between you and death time and time again. She takes the consequences for you as often as you do wrong. When the consequence cannot be avoided; Mercy provides mercy and tempers the punishment so that you can bear it. She possesses WonderWoman qualities as she leaves everyone she blesses to wonder what they've done to deserve her blessings. Mercy has her own weapon that compels others to tell the truth about the predicament they were in and would still be in if it had not been for Mercy. Wonder as they may, one can never identify something that warrants Mercy's favor.

Her thoughts are always bursting with compassion, love and leniency. Mercy's mission twenty four hours a day, seven days a week is to ensure that no one gets what they deserve! Mercy is sensitive to the needs of everyone she meets as she is compassionate, empathetic, sympathetic and understanding of our circumstances though she does not excuse the wilful deeds we commit that request the immediate need for her.

Because of Mercy:

Mercy makes you *mindful* of your failures, your limits, and your lack. When you've been shown mercy, you become keenly aware of why mercy needed to be extended to you. There is an overwhelming sense of relief, as in your periphery you see the demise, the destruction, the disaster, you were undeservedly and unbeknowingly spared from. You experience an elation that is so overpowering and so awesome that you are careful not to take it for granted, but to instead thank God incessantly for his extension of mercy to you.

When mercy is extended to you, you become *merciful.* You begin to seek ways to extend mercy to others. You unapologetically aspire to extend the same amount of mercy to others that was extended to you. You want to have others to share the benefit of mercy, to feel the emotions that result from being spared and rescued beit from a pothole on the road sure to render you a flat tire, or from the big rig that strayed into your lane at top speed, or from the unemployment line, or the near destruction of your home, or from the unavoidable natural disaster that strikes without warning.

You naturally begin to extend mercy to those you meet, those you work with, those you worship with, those who love you, those who despise you. You learn by the experience of having mercy extended to you how to be merciful. So you would let the person pulling up on your right side at top speed in traffic in front of you though they do not have the right of way. You begin to restrain from responding in kind to someone who is unjustly degrading or embarrassing you. Extending mercy to others makes you happy, makes you more content with yourself, and yes, I believe that extensions of mercy to others over time will have mercy extended back to you.

Modesty is a byproduct of Mercy. Not, meekness, but modesty. There is a sense of humility, that mercy evokes in you. You become very aware, when extended mercy, that your life is not your own, you have no real say in the decisions that you 'make', no hope to save yourself from life's unpredictability. You are but a pawn, on the great chessboard of life, and if it were not for the mercy extended to you by God Almighty, you would not be. You wear the cloak of modesty with an awareness that it is a cloak you earned in place of the consequence you deserved.

This cloak compels you to show compassion to all that you meet, it inspires you to feel as they feel, empathize with others and to completely understand their sense of elation that they were mercifully dealt with. This cloak protects you from the insensitivity of arrogance or vainful pride. Instead the cloak covers you with the modesty that someone who is repentant, contemplative, delivered and spared would assume.

As a friend:

Girlfriend Mercy is the friend that thinks of everything to make our lives easier, more liveable, comfortable and peaceful. Mercy is the one that takes note of all that we've done and then acts like it never happened.

She is compassionate, forgiving, easy to please, discerning, kind, patient, avoids strife and seeks peace.

Mercy makes her presence known, not in a pompous manner, but because she exudes compassion and forgiveness; two easily recognizable characteristics. Mercy is sympathetic to her friends' feelings, emotions, thoughts, behaviors and consequences. She displays high degrees of tolerance. She will tolerate your disregard, disinterest, mistakes and flaws; meeting them with high degrees of empathy and sensitivity.

Regardless of what you do, Mercy forgives. She does not hold grudges, chooses to forget the wrongs done to her and moves on from the ills she suffered. Mercy suffers long and seeks to, through a steady measure of compassion and forgiveness, have her closest girlfriends to emulate her behaviors in their own lives.

Mercy is the girlfriend that listens to everything you have to say about how someone may have destroyed you emotionally, disrupted your concept of your self worth and violated your trust. After listening, she encourages you to overlook and forgive the flaws in and of others. Incredulously, she implores you to try to understand why you may have been violated, why your feelings may have been hurt, how you can find the way to forgive and then insist that you extend mercy to those that have offended. Refusing to relinquish her power to the offender, Mercy insists that you bury any feelings of resentment, deny the need for revenge and restore the feelings of goodwill and affection and then graciously extend to them the undeserved arm of grace.

Girlfriend to Girlfriend:

- Always give thanks for our friendship.
- Always show mercy as you would want it shown to you.
- Remember that no one deserves me, yet I am available to everyone.
- Be merciful to others.
- Don't hold grudges; they hold you back from your potential.
- Forgive those who've offended you, thereby freeing yourself.

Mercy in Quotation Marks:

"Granted leniency and pardon though unworthy."

Her Hashtags:

#missionclemency
#undeservedpardon
#grudgefree
#forgivenessforall
#inmycorner

<u>Your Turn</u>

_____
_____
_____

Recognizing Mercy:
- Relationships of every kind (home, school, career, church, personal, professional)
- Avoided accidents
- Safe travel
- Spared life
- Safe delivery of a child
- Shelter through life's storms
- Avoided sickness or disease

<u>Your Turn</u>

- _____
- _____
- _____

Acknowledgement:
    It is because of Mercy that I am not consumed. I know that God loves me because of how Mercy treats me. She is so kind to me; she knows the inner woes and transgressions of my heart and soul and still is compassionate to me. Mercy keeps me centered on God's providence and protection. For it is only because of Him, that I am not consumed.

Reflection on Mercy:

1. Your thoughts to or about Mercy -

   _____
   _____
   _____
   _____
   _____

2. Has God ever shown up for you like he had for the two widows of mercy referenced in the Bible? Relate the experience.

   _____
   _____
   _____
   _____
   _____

3. When was the last time you extended mercy to someone? How difficult was it to do so? What did you have to deny in yourself in order to grant mercy?

   _____
   _____
   _____
   _____

4. Justify the statement, God is a God of mercy.

   _____
   _____
   _____
   _____

5. Which is the most powerful of the siblings, Grace or Mercy? Why do you say so?

_____
_____
_____
_____
_____

6. Mercy does not require anything for you to get her attention. What should be a natural response after you have requested and received Mercy?

_____
_____
_____
_____
_____

7. Mercy is forgiving, but at times does not eliminate the consequences for our actions. Why is this so?

_____
_____
_____
_____
_____

8. Make a list of the sins or actions for which God has granted you mercy. For each one, what would have been a possible consequence if God had not mercifully stepped in on your behalf?

_____
_____
_____
_____

9. Write a thank you note to Mercy.

   _____
   _____
   _____
   _____
   _____

10. Mercy is like the Sheerah read of in the Bible and likened to the 1980s fictional super *she*ro, She-rah. She swoops in as a superhero would and saves us from sure destruction. What might her powers be?

    _____
    _____
    _____
    _____
    _____

Assignment:
1. Find a homeless person or someone in need and give them a few dollars; buy them breakfast or lunch.
2. Donate to the homeless shelter or second hand store.
3. Send a small gift to your child's teacher.
4. Forgive someone who's wronged you.
5. Thank God for the mercy extended to you and those you love.
6. Adopt an animal from the local animal shelter.
7. Write a note to a girlfriend telling her what mercy means to you.
8. Perform a chore for someone today without them asking you to do so.
9. Book a pedicure for yourself; your feet will thank you for it.
10. Shorten a punishment doled out to your child though justified.

Girlfriend Charity

Caring

Humane

gr**A**cious

f**R**uit of the Spirit

g**I**ving

Tolerant

sisterl**Y** love

Charity

Definition: love

Origin: Late Old English

Meaning: Brotherly Love

Bible Verses:
1 Corinthians 13:4-8
4 Charity suffereth long, and is kind; charity envieth not; charity vaunteth not itself, is not puffed up,
5 Doth not behave itself unseemly, seeketh not her own, is not easily provoked, thinketh no evil;
6 Rejoiceth not in iniquity, but rejoiceth in the truth;
7 Beareth all things, believeth all things, hopeth all things, endureth all things.
8 Charity never faileth: but whether there be prophecies, they shall fail; whether there be tongues, they shall cease; whether there be knowledge, it shall vanish away.

1 Corinthians 13:13
And now abideth faith, hope, charity, these three; but the greatest of these is charity.

Bible Reference:
Luke 10 v. 30-37
In the well-known story of the Good Samaritan, it is told that a man who was traveling between cities, was robbed, beaten and left for dead. A priest came by; crossed to the other side of the road and did not help the man. A Levite came on by, looked at him, kept on walking and did not help. A Samaritan came upon the man, demonstrated charity in the truest sense of the word as he gave to the afflicted, sick and poor. The traveler was all of these after the unfortunate encounter with the thieves.

Women of Charity in the Bible:
- *Dorcas* - earned fame and prestige for her dress-making. She was also an avid philanthropist and she gave away everything she had and could, in love, to those in need and to the honor and glory of God. (Acts 9:36-43)
- *Harlot mother, (there were two),* because of the love for her son would rather live without her child than him severed in two because of the untrue word of her callous companion spoken before King Solomon that claimed the remaining living child was hers. (1 Kings 3)

- *Jehosheba,* a princess married to high priest, courageously stole her nephew Joash to preserve his life and the royal seed of the line of Judah. (2 Kings 11:2; 2 Chronicles 22:11)
- *Joanna,* having being shown grace and mercy being healed from her infirmities, was numbered as one of Jesus' 12 and ministered to Jesus by giving of her plenty, in love, to meet his and his disciples' needs. (Luke 8 1-3)
- *Jochebed,* mother of Moses, because of her love for her son devised a clever plan to have his life spared so that he could become one of the greatest leaders to the people of Israel in the Bible. Exodus 1; 2:1-11; 6:20; Numbers 26:59; Hebrews 11:23
- *Leah,* Jacob's first wife, named her first four sons and testified of her love for God by their given names; Behold a son, Hearing, Joined, and Praise. (Genesis 29; 30; 49:31; Ruth 4:11)
- *Lydia* showed love to Paul and Silas upon their release from prison. She was hospitable to those in need by housing them in her home; caring for them physically and spiritually. Her home became a gathering place for believers; perhaps the first church. Acts 16:12-15, 40; Philippians 1:1-10
- *Martha,* was gracious and hospitable. She loved and served Jesus, her brother Lazarus and her sister Mary. (Luke 10:38-41; John 11; 12:1-3)
- *Mary,* the mother of Jesus, loved her first and virgin-born son more than any mother has ever loved her child, in that she gave him up to die for our sins. (Luke 2 v 7)
- *Mary Magdalene,* so indebted to Christ for her sanity and her life, she became a devout disciple of Christ. She was there at the foot of the cross during the crucifixion and at the tomb to announce that He was no longer dead but risen. (Luke 23:49)
- *Mary of Bethany,* for her alabaster box of ointment with which she washed Jesus' feet. (Luke 10:38-41; John 11; 12:1-3)
- *Noah's wife* was a constant source of encouragement to him in his old and ridicule filled age as he built an ark by God's command for the impending and promised yet not-seen flood. (Genesis 6:18; 7:1, 7, 13; 8:16, 18)
- *Phebe* was a sister to Paul in the ministry and is considered the first deaconess of the christian church. She served as a loving and hospitable helper to Paul, those in the ministry and the church. (Romans 16:1, 2)
- *Pharaoh's daughter*, the female savior of the people of Israel showed love to Moses treating him like a son in the palace of Pharaoh. (Exodus 2:5-10; Acts 7:21; Hebrews 11:24)
- Saul's sons by Milcah and *Rizpah* (7 in all) were hung in revenge for Saul breaking an oath he'd made with the Gibeonites. All seven bodies were lovingly

guarded by Rizpah to disallow the bodies to be ravished by natural scavengers until the rain came, after which the bodies were buried. (2 Samuel 3:7; 21:8-14)
- *Ruth*, daugher in law to a bitter Naomi demonstrated charity to Naomi, by refusing to be severed from her even after presented the opportunity. Ruth had befriended Naomi, her mother in law, declared Naomi's God to be hers and refused to abandon her when it would have been much simpler to do so. Ruth, later fell in love with and married Boaz. (The Book of Ruth)
- *Wise Hearted women*, served the church by joyfully, willingly and without reward hand making woven cloths for the completion of the Tabernacle of the Lord. (Exodus 35 vs 22-29)

About Charity:

Not intending to be redundant, but Charity loves you. Charity loves unconditionally. Charity is Love. She is not concerned with your stature, your appearance, your wealth, your status, your career, your position in the church, your age, your weight, nothing about you could change Charity's opinion about you, nor have her to love you any less. Thoughts of you by Charity engenders love.

Charity likes to comfort, heal, give, share, support, encourage and love. She cherishes the opportunity to have everyone that experiences her to be better, love harder and love everyone. Simply put, through her immense power and transforming reach, Love supplies your every emotional need; be it self esteem, motivation, comfort, peace, hope, determination, healing, solace, etc. Love beareth all things.

Everyone agrees that Charity is loyal. She would have to be as she has locked herself away in our hearts; refusing to be coaxed, commanded or cajoled out of her most sacred space. Love prepares for war with detractors like sin, death, separation, abuse, disregard, contempt, hatred. She insists on loving those who are the most unlovable and by that singular act; she wins them to the Love of Christ. Love is perfect. God is love.

Charity's feelings, thoughts and actions all coincide to fulfill her mission which is to show you what love is, show you how to love God, yourself and others and to compel you to share the unboundable love cultivated within you with everyone you meet.

Because of Charity:

Love begets Love. Simply put, when you are shown love, you show love. Vice versa, when you show love, love is shown to you. It therefore is a fact that when you have a friendship with Charity, you become **charitable.** Charity begins the reciprocal relationship of giving to get. How so? Well, when one gives with a charitable spirit, they are able to get immense and immeasurable rewards; rewards that are quite intangible, they are difficult to describe but a pleasure to experience. What you get from giving charitably pulls at your heartstrings, it touches your emotions, unplugs your tear ducts and inspires you to touch others in the manner that you were impacted.

Because He first loved us and showed His love toward us. We strive daily to emulate His love and **choose Christlike virtues.** We make a conscious effort because of His divine love shown to us, to do as He would do. We give attention and assistance to children, the homeless, the needy; those worse off than we are. We turn the other cheek when wronged. We remind others of God's insatiable love toward us. We show evidences of God's love to everyone we meet. We show our love for God to him, by tithing, serving others and the church, by caring for and shepherding our family, by reciprocating His love to us by accepting His plan of salvation. We obey the greatest commandment of all, we; 'Love the Lord our God with all of our heart and with all our soul and with all our mind and with all our strength.' We love our neighbor as we do ourselves' (Mark 12: 30-31).

There is no other emotion that is as strong and as transforming as love. Love is a supercharged **change agent.** Love changes hearts, minds, and intent. Love transforms a sinner to a saint, an evil person to one equipped for glory, a persecutor to a preacher, a person bound for hell to one boasting of a heavenly crown. Love is a change agent. A prayer prayed in and with love is heard by Love, for Christ is love. The transformative power of Love is supernatural. The depth, breadth and scope of this supernatural change agent is inconceivable by humans, it is redemptive, just, praise-worthy, it is humble, transformative, it is indescribable, it is intangible, though not unattainable, it is God.

As a friend:

Charity is immediately recognized and acknowledged, as she enters a room, simply by the beauty she possesses. She is compassionate, modest, chaste, patient, fair, celebrates truth, has a strong belief system, hopeful, highly successful and enduring.

Despite being a beautiful woman, inside and out, Charity is not vain or arrogant. She is heralded as the greatest of her siblings, Faith and Hope. She is the kind of friend that though she unwillingly demands all the attention from others when you go out together, she does not flaunt it but instead tries to spread the wealth by drawing you into the conversation, bringing you into the dialogue or leaving the room so the conversation would not focus on her but rather on you.

She has a high tolerance for provocation; so you can say or do almost anything to Charity and she will not lash out at you. She assumes positive intentions and keeps it moving. She delights in the truth, is honest, frank and tactful. She is the friend every girlfriend needs. She won't be on the fence about how you look, what you should wear, whether you should dump your boyfriend, ignore the harassment or quit the job. Instead she'll give you her advice with her love, care and concern for you being foremost in her mind.

Charity would never have to be reminded to say something if she was to see something. She is her brother and sister's keeper. She demonstrates brotherly (and sisterly) love and sees the world through the filter of Luke 6:31; And as ye would that men should do to you, do ye also to them likewise.

Charity is the friend you want in your corner, the one that is going to motivate you, keep you motivated, support you through every situation, encourage you, pray for you, correct you, believe in you when others do not, care for you, give you the shirt off of her back literally, comfort you back to health if sick, feed you if hungry, and bandage your wounds if afflicted. Charity is your cheerleader!

Girlfriend to Girlfriend:

- Be sure you have a clear picture of what love is.
- Love yourself completely first and then love everyone else the way you want to be loved.
- Ensure that you are not substituting what you know love to be for what you have.
- Remember, love does not hurt.

Charity in Quotation Marks:

"The purest, most transparent and necessary affection."

Her Hashtags:

#longsuffering
#noenvy
#thinksnoevil
#slowtoprovoke
#neverfails
#sisterlylove
#greatestvirtue
#loveforall
#paidinfull

Your Turn

\# _____
\# _____
\# _____

Recognizing Charity:
- Acts of Humanity
- Giving to the poor, afflicted, sick, less fortunate
- Giving the right of way in traffic
- Support
- Modesty
- Chastity
- Frank conversation
- Celebrations
- Success

Your Turn

- _____
- _____
- _____

Acknowledgement:
The world has changed and is changing, sadly not for the better. There seems to be so much that is going wrong in the world today. Charity renews my hope in humanity. Charity reminds me that there is good in the world and that we should emulate and spread the good that Charity possesses and that good should begin with me.

Reflection on Charity:

1. Your thoughts to or about Charity -

_____
_____
_____
_____

2. Charity is named as the greatest of the triad in 1 Corinthians 13 v. 13. Why do you think this is so?

   _____
   _____
   _____
   _____

3. One of my girlfriends is a modern-day Ruth; serving her mother-in-law years after her marriage ended though for different reasons than Ruth's did. Do you believe love is always rewarded? Do you believe every woman has a Boaz? Why or why not?

   _____
   _____
   _____
   _____

4. What characteristics of love outlined in 1 Corinthians 13:4-8 have you demonstrated in your relationships? Which ones do you need to work on?

   _____
   _____
   _____
   _____

5. Charity means brotherly love; for the purpose of this text; 'sisterly love'. How do you demonstrate charity currently and to whom? Think of and commit to one other way to demonstrate charity to someone.

   _____
   _____
   _____

6. Is it possible to love others without loving yourself? How?

7. Over and over, secular artists have belted the lyrics declaring what the world needs now. I declare, it is what the world has always needed; LOVE. Do you think there is love in the world today? Where do you see it? How is it demonstrated? Do you think there is enough love in the world today? Why or why not?

8. Often women have a more difficult time recognizing what love is not than they should. This is probably because they have a misrepresentation of what love is from their past or their present is currently misrepresenting love. Think of your life, specifically its relationships; make a list of the things that are not love.

9. Considering question 8, what will you do about your list?

_____
_____
_____
_____
_____

10. Ignorance to how someone wants or needs to be loved is often the culprit for broken relationships. Draw a heart of a large piece of paper; cut the heart into puzzle pieces. On each puzzle piece, write one way you need or want to be loved. Consider making several puzzles for each of your different types of relationships. Have those with whom you are in a loving relationship to put the puzzles together to discover how you need or want to be loved. Begin your list below:

_____   _____
_____   _____
_____   _____
_____   _____

Assignment:
1. Volunteer at a homeless shelter or soup kitchen.
2. Give cases of copy paper, notebook paper, pencils, school supplies to your local school.
3. Attend and participate in a PTO meeting at your child's school.
4. Love someone who has not shown love, affection or care to you.
5. Pack your spouse's lunch and include a loving note.
6. Take your pet on a long walk.
7. Post a 'love' message on facebook.
8. Exchange 'love puzzles' (number 10 above) with those you share relationships with.
9. Show yourself some self-love; do something for yourself that makes you happy.
10. Show love to someone else; how they like it.

Girlfriend Faith

hopeFul

deAd without works

belIef, void of proof

Trust in God

wHat we walk by

Faith

Definition: belief and trust in God; firm belief in something for which there is no proof.

Origin: Latin

Meaning: Trust and Faith

Bible Verses:
Matthew 21 v 21
Jesus answered and said unto them, Verily I say unto you, If ye have faith, and doubt not, ye shall not only do this which is done to the fig tree, but also if ye shall say unto this mountain, Be thou removed, and be thou cast into the sea; it shall be done.

Hebrews 11 v 1
Now faith is the substance of things hoped for, the evidence of things not seen.

2 Corinthians 5 v 7
For we walk by faith, not by sight.

Matthew 17 v 20
And Jesus said unto them, Because of your unbelief: for verily I say unto you, If ye have faith as a grain of mustard seed, ye shall say unto this mountain, Remove hence to yonder place; and it shall remove; and nothing shall be impossible unto you.

Bible Reference:
Genesis 22

After waiting for more than a lifetime, or so it seemed, Abraham and Sarah finally benefitted from the promise God made to them, by having a son; Isaac. Abraham and Sarah must have thought with the birth of Isaac that God's test of their faith was complete. A few years later, God tested their (Abraham's) faith again, by asking him to sacrifice his only son in obedience to God. Abraham obediently made the trek to the mountain and prepared Isaac to be sacrificed. Certainly, he could not understand it, certainly he questioned God, but he literally 'walked by faith' and by his faith the mountain though it stood still, the need to sacrifice Isaac was removed.

Women of Faith in the Bible:

- *Abigail* - trusted God to raise a godly son though married to an ungodly man.
- *Achsah* - looked for great things through the promise of God's land.
- *Azubah* - mother of King Jehoshaphat, a commendable king. Her love for the Lord played a great role in the life of her son.
- *Candace* - witnessed to by a Eunuch, embraced the Christian faith.
- *Claudia* - woman of Gentile origin who heard and believed the Gospel.
- *Elisabeth* - a righteous woman who along with her husband walked in all the commandments of the Lord.
- *Eunice* - a woman of God that from birth nurtured and admonished Timothy, her son in the fear and admonition of the Lord. (Acts 16:1-3; 2 Timothy 1:5; 3:14, 15; 4:5)
- *Euodias and Syntyche* after their conversions became co-laborers with Paul.
- *Hannah*, the favored wife of Elkanah could not bare children, suffered at the tongue of Elkanah's second wife and was after prayer and supplication granted mercy and was given Samuel who she promised to return to the Lord and she did.
- *Huldah* was consulted when the lost book of the law was found. Huldah's prophetic message and the reading of the law brought about a revival in the land. (2 Kings 22:14-20; 2 Chronicles 34:22-33)
- *Ichabod's mother*, a faithful believer, died on her deathbed after naming her child and learning that the Ark of the Covenant had been taken, signaling the absence of God's glory. (1 Samuel 4:19-22)
- *Leah,* Jacob's first wife, bore him six sons which were to be six of the twelve tribes of Israel. Though despised by her younger sister, Jacob's second wife, she remained faithful to her husband and to God. The naming of her first four sons testified of this as their names mean; Behold a son, Hearing, Joined, and Praise. (Genesis 29; 30; 49:31; Ruth 4:11)
- *Jecholiah,* wife to a king and mother of a king, sought God and her son did right in the sight of the Lord as king. (2 Kings 15:2; 2 Chronicles 26:3)
- *Jedidah,* mother of Josiah who became king at 8 years old and ruled for 31 years, testament to his mother's faith and connection to God. (2 Kings 22:1, 2)
- *Jehosheba,* a princess married to a high priest, by faith stole her nephew Joash to preserve his life and the royal seed of the line of Judah. (2 Kings 11:2; 2 Chronicles 22:11)
- *Joanna,* having being shown grace and mercy being healed from her infirmities, was numbered as one of Jesus' faithful disciples and ministered to Jesus by giving of her plenty to meet Jesus' and his disciples' needs. (Luke 8 1-3)

- *Jochebed,* mother of Moses, by faith, devised a clever plan to have his life spared so that he could become one of the greatest leaders to the people of Israel in the Bible. Exodus 1; 2:1-11; 6:20; Numbers 26:59; Hebrews 11:23
- *Lois,* grandmother of Timothy was won to Christ by the ministry of Paul. She, Timothy and Timothy's mother were stalwart believers in the Christ of whom Paul preached. (2 Timothy 1:5)
- *Lydia,* an astute business woman, was well-known for her sale of purple dye. She sought God daily for grace and knowledge to run her business. She, upon her conversion, told others in her household about God who were likewise converted and baptized. (Acts 16 v 14)
- *Manoah's wife and Samson's mother,* patiently waited on the Lord for him to end her barrenness and grant her a child. God appeared to both she and Manoah assuring them that they would receive a very special son. By faith, they believed. Granted Samson, Manoah's wife became a joyous mother of a future judge of Israel. (Judges 13; 14:2-5; Hebrews 11:32)
- *Mary,* the mother of Jesus, believed wholeheartedly in whom she was charged to bore. She believed in the fulfillment of prophecy though it would bring pain to hers, a mother's heart. She believed that not only would Christ leave, but that He would return to claim us unto Himself. (Matthew 1; 2; 12:46; Luke 1; 2; John 2:1-11; 19:25; Acts 1:14)
- *Mary Magdalene,* after being liberated from demons, and clothed in her right mind; became an astute woman of faith and a devoted disciple of Christ. (Matthew 27:56, 61; 28:1; Mark 15:40, 47; 16:1-19; Luke 8:2; 24:10; John 19:25; 20:1-18.)
- *Mary of Bethany,* was a faithful follower of Christ. She washed Jesus' feet after sitting and listening intently at his feet to learn more of him. (Luke 10:38-41; John 11; 12:1-3)
- *Miriam,* sister of Moses and Aaron and the first poetess in the Bible, led the women in a song of praise and joy for God's faithfulness toward them at The Red Sea. (Exodus 15 v. 20 and 21)
- *Naaman's wife's maid,* shared her faith with everyone she met, including her slave owner. She believed that the prophet Elisha could heal Naaman of the undesirous leprosy; which he did after Naaman's obedience to dip seven times in the Jordan River. (2 Kings 5:1-19)
- *Phebe* was a sister to Paul in the ministry and is considered to be the first deaconess of the christian church. She served as a loving and hospitable helper to Paul, and others in the church. (Romans 16:1, 2)
- *Puah and Shiprah,* two Egyptian midwives who were in charge of a large number of midwives directed to kill the Israelite males upon their births. The women

together determined that true to their faith they could not do such and claimed that the babies were born before they could get to them, thereby sparing their lives. (Exodus 15 v. 1-21).

- *Rahab,* hid the men of God with an assured peace that she was doing the right thing and that her faith in practice would be rewarded in that she would be spared from certain destruction. She is one of only two women who is designated as an example of faith in the great cloud of witnesses. (Joshua 2:1, 3; 6:17-25)
- *Sarah* - showed faith and obedience while trusting in and telling of God's promises. She is one of only two women who is designated as an example of faith in the great cloud of witnesses.
- *Salome,* wife of Zebedee, mother of James and John two of Jesus' disciples was faithful to Christ and requested that her sons be seated on the right and left hands of God. God honored her request differently than perhaps she would have liked by allowing James to be the first apostolic martyr and John to be the last.
- *Sarah* was 90 years old when she conceived a son to her long wedded husband, Abraham. Until God appeared to Abraham, they were childless. The conception of Isaac was one of faith as Sarah was well advanced beyond childbearing age. (Genesis 17 and 18)
- *Syro-Phoenician Woman,* pressed her way to Jesus so that she could have her daughter healed from demons that were possessing her. Jesus did not fail to reward her faith by giving her the desires of her heart. (Matthew 15:21-28; Mark 7:24-30)
- *Tryphena and Tryphosa* were consistent and faithful laborers in the christian church. (Romans 16 v 12)
- *Widow of Zarephath,* housed and served the prophet Elijah. When her son died and was resurrected, she came to believe in the God of whom Elijah prophesied. (1 Kings 17:8-24)
- Widow with two mites, gave out of her poverty to God's treasury. (Luke 21 1:1-4)
- *Woman of Shunem,* after receiving the promise of and later the receipt of a son in her old age. The son died and Elisha at the request of his grief stricken and believing mother restored him to life. (2 Kings 4:8-37; 8:1-6)
- *Woman with the issue of blood,* suffered for 12 years and was healed instantaneously by her faith and action to touch the hem of Jesus' garment. (Matthew 9:20-22; Mark 5:25-34; Luke 8:43-48)
- *Zibiah,* wife of King Ahaziah and a faithful and Godly mother of King Joash who served for 40 years. (2 Kings 12:1; 2 Chronicles 24:1)

About Faith:

Faith is immovable by emotions. Whereas 'emotional' would most likely be one of the most named adjectives to describe females; it is an inaccurate description for Faith. Faith holds on to her convictions, holds fast to her hope and is not swayed by the feelings of sadness or despair as the days turn into weeks, then months, and then years without an affirmative answer from God. She is not distracted, nor angered by the naysayers who whisper behind her back or speak ill of her in front of her face. She remains focused and level-headed convinced that if she were to lose her cool, she would forfeit her reward.

Faith thinks incessantly about the attainment of everything believed for. She works at blinding people to the pain, fear, anger, depression, and apprehension they would feel as their faith is tested so that their thoughts are always centered firmly on the attainment of what they trust for and Who they trust in.

Others admire how resolute Faith is. She is decisive and steadfast, an independent thinker, a go-getter and a goal achiever. They envy her ability to go against the odds, and blindly remain committed without an inkling or indication and certainly no proof of the reward, nor when it will come.

Because of Faith:

Faith compels you to be **faithful**. Faithful in the 'committed' sense of the word as well as faithful in the 'full of faith' sense of the word. Because of faith, you will be committed to giving your tithe, attending church, feeding the hungry, caring for the sick, selecting and serving in a ministry, ensuring that your bills are paid, seeing that your children are well cared for and attend the very best schools. You will be committed.

You will also be 'full of faith' as you will trust that the school will be the best for your child, that their caregivers will be kind and fair, that you will make the money to pay your bills, that your service in ministry will be beneficial to those you serve, that the sick will one day get well, that the hungry will one day no longer be hungry, that your attendance at church will be a display of your devotion to God and a testimony of His goodness to someone else, that you will always have money to meet your needs when you pay your tithe and that the tithe will be used to God's glory. You will be full of faith.

You will be **fervent in prayer** because faith is the substance hoped for and the evidence of things not seen. It is impossible to have faith without being prayerful. Prayer is the fuel for our faith. We could not remain faithful if we did not pray like we should. We have to have an implicit and sustained trust in God, we have to petition Him for His favor, His mercy, His grace and the fulfillment of His promises. We know what God has promised us, defense (Exodus 14 v.14); long life (Exodus 20 v. 12); strength and power (Isaiah 40 v. 29); help (Isaiah 41 v. 13); protection (Isaiah 54 v. 17); and plans to prosper you and not harm you, plans to give you a hope and a future (Jeremiah

29 v. 11). In order to redeem these promises, we must be obedient, read and obey the Bible, humble ourselves, turn from our wicked ways and be fervent in prayer.

It is true that Faith = Favor. When you are faithful, you will be **favored.** It is impossible to be faithful and not gain God's favor. Favor is the reward for our faithfulness to Him, to His Word and to His will. You will know that you are favored because of your faith because you will experience overflow that you will not have room to receive; for eyes have not seen - evidence of it being a result of your faith.

As a friend:

Faith is the friend that lives up to her name. She is faithful, she trusts in and believes in God. She believes that everything happens for a reason and for everything there is a purpose though she does not know what it is; neither does she care. She unapologetically trusts and believes in God. She is therefore carefree, a free thinker, a free spirit, confident that God's got her and everything that pertains to her and her girlfriends.

She is not analytical, but instead is a big picture girl. She is uninhibited by the details, or the reasons. She does not concern herself with the why but is concerned with who knows the details.

Faith is the go-getter of the girlfriend group, she is boundary-blind! She is a risk-taker, she throws everything away in reckless abandon however is not careless! She just believes that there are no boundaries to whatever she puts her mind to. Though she and all of her closest friends are successful; she challenges her current successes by thinking about something bigger, then simply sets out to accomplish it. Faith is the kind of friend that pushes you out of your comfort zone; cheers you on, encourages you to reach higher, do more, accomplish more, be more; not because it looks like you can but because she believes you can!

Girlfriend to Girlfriend:
- Have faith in God.
- When you and your faith are tried; remember that Jesus was tried.
- It's when it appears that there is no hope in a situation, that God does His best work.
- Never take your hand out of mine.
- I am the fuel for your dreams, your hopes, your desires and your restoration.
- Everything will work out for your good.
- Stand in there! Don't give up! Don't quit!

Faith in Quotation Marks:

"Ludicrous belief in spite of negligible proof."

Her Hashtags:

#faithisblind
#nodoubt
#nofear
#boundaryblind
#unapolgeticbelief
#hopedfor
#notseen

<u>Your Turn</u>

_____
_____
_____

Recognizing Faith:
- Going for the job you are least qualified for.
- Going for a job you are qualified for.
- Applying for a loan with poor or no credit.
- Hoping for a child while barren.
- Believing your husband will return from another woman's bed.
- Believing your failing or failed marriage can be repaired.
- Starting a degree program.
- Wanting a cure for an incurable disease.
- Desiring healing for your child.
- Believing for a financial blessing.

<u>Your Turn</u>

- _____
- _____
- _____

Acknowledgement:

I can't do anything without Faith. She and I have a relationship that requires that though we don't see each other every day, we must communicate. I must call her by name, ensuring that she and I maintain our friendship, and are always close to each other. Our intimate trust relationship is so powerful, so catalytic, so monumental, so 'faithFULL', and so mountain moving!

Reflection on Faith:

1. Your thoughts to or about Faith-

   _____

   _____

   _____

   _____

   _____

2. The woman with the issue of blood is one of the Bible stories of faith that I never tire of hearing. She mobilized faith, literally, by pressing her way to Jesus and making the move to touch the hem of his garment to be made whole. What in your life needs to be mobilized by faith? Outline a plan to mobilize your faith.

   _____

   _____

   _____

   _____

   _____

   _____

   _____

   _____

   _____

3. There are a large number of women mentioned as being women of faith; some being women of other categories as well. What does this say about women? In general? In relationships? In the church? In the ministry?

___

4. Critique the following quote about faith: "Ludicrous belief in spite of negligible proof."

___

5. Defend our walk by faith and not by sight. Does God ever grant us sight of what can be and what will be when we walk by faith?

___

6. Judge; is faith always rewarded?

_____
_____
_____
_____
_____

7. Complete the chart below to make a list of your 'mountains' that you've encountered along life's journey, identify what must be done in addition to prayer to have them moved and plan your faith walk under, around, through or over the mountain.

Mountain	What must be done

8. Write a Faith Mantra; perhaps yours is already written for you in one of the Bible verses you've committed to memory concerning faith. If not, consider writing and committing one to memory that you could recite daily to remember your girlfriend Faith.

_____
_____
_____
_____
_____

9. The armor of God includes a shield of faith. Label the shield with the protective items that would be used as protection in life's battles.

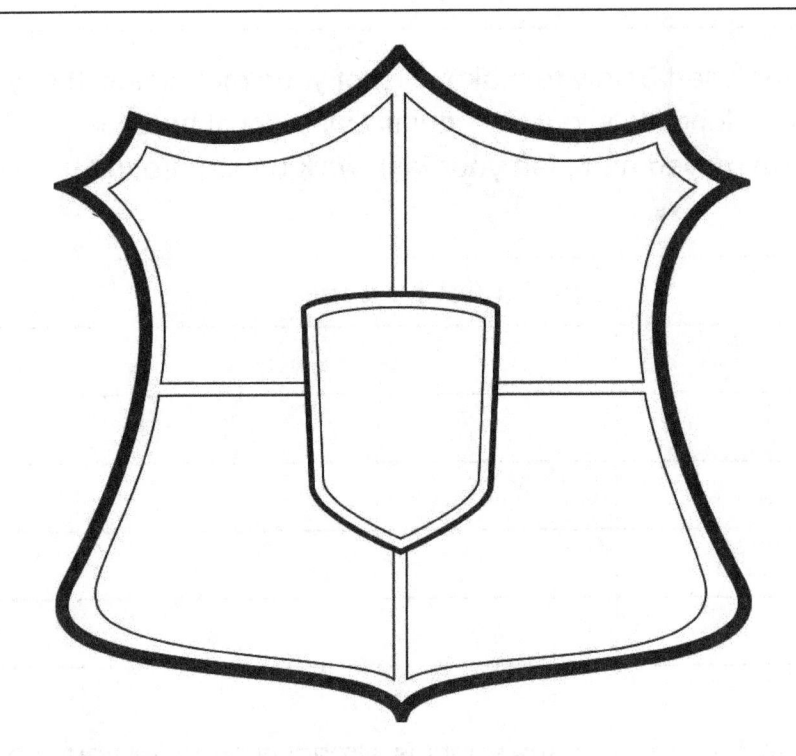

_____
_____
_____
_____

10. When should Faith and you be no longer friends?

_____
_____
_____
_____

Assignment:
1. Pray with or for someone today that their faith will remain strong.
2. Encourage someone to meet their goals, keep their head up, stay strong.
3. Pray for your child's teacher.
4. Trust God in and for everything.
5. Thank someone for the faith they had in you; to give you a job, to assist you in some way, etc.

6. Let someone know you have faith in them, their idea, their goals, etc.
7. Commit anew to something that you'd recently had your doubts about but once believed in.
8. Keep an optimistic outlook regarding something that looks like it is not going to happen.
9. Read your Bible asking God to show you something in his word to bolster your faith.
10. Tell someone about Christ.

Girlfriend Hope

Has faith

Optimistic

Prays without ceasing

Expects with confidence

Hope

Definition: to want something to happen or be true; to expect with confidence.

Origin: English

Meaning: Trust, Faith

Bible Verses:

Romans 12:12 - Rejoicing in hope; patient in tribulation; continuing instant in prayer;

Romans 5 v 2-5
2 By whom also we have access by faith into this grace wherein we stand, and rejoice in hope of the glory of God.
3 And not only [so], but we glory in tribulations also: knowing that tribulation worketh patience;
4 And patience, experience; and experience, hope:
5 And hope maketh not ashamed; because the love of God is shed abroad in our hearts by the Holy Ghost which is given unto us.

Jeremiah 17:7 - Blessed [is] the man that trusteth in the LORD, and whose hope the LORD is.

Psalm 130 v 5
I wait for the LORD, my soul doth wait, and in his word do I hope.

Bible Reference:
1 Samuel
     Hannah was a woman full of hope for something that she had every reason not to be hopeful for. She was hopeful that God would answer her prayer for a son. Wife to Elkanah who had two wives, Hannah suffered the shame of having no children, though Peninah the other wife bore Elkanah children. Hannah had hope that God would one day open up her womb. Hannah promised God that when she received a son, she would not cut the child's hair and that she would return him to God for His service.

Though thought to be drunk by Eli who watched her pray, and the inevitable and painstaking passage of time and unending ridicule by Peninah, Hannah remained hopeful. Because of her consistent hope and trust in God, God answered Hannah's prayers and rewarded her hope with a son, Samuel.

Women of Hope in the Bible:
- *Hannah*, the favored wife of Elkanah could not bare children, suffered at the tongue of Elkanah's second wife and after prayer and supplication was rewarded for her hope and was given Samuel.
- *Jochebed,* mother of Moses, devised a clever plan to have his life spared so that he could become one of the greatest leaders to the people of Israel in the Bible. Exodus 1; 2:1-11; 6:20; Numbers 26:59; Hebrews 11:23
- *Leah,* Jacob's first wife, remained hopeful that Jacob would love her as he did Rachel. The naming of her first four sons testified of this as their names mean; Behold a son, Hearing, Joined, and Praise. (Genesis 29; 30; 49:31; Ruth 4:11)
- *Rhoda,* the handmaid to Mary of Jerusalem, and the others in the house were hopeful that Peter would be released from prison. (Acts 12 v 1-19)
- *Salome,* wife of Zebedee, mother of James and John two of Jesus' disciples was hopeful that her sons would be seated on the right and left hands of God. God honored her request differently than perhaps she would have liked by allowing James to be the first apostolic martyr and John to be the last.
- *Tamar*, hoping to be of the line of Judah gained her ancestry to the line of Christ by engaging in an incestuous relationship with Judah, her father in law of two of Tamar's former husbands. (Genesis 38 v. 6-30)

About Hope:
Hope feels deeply. She is very sensitive to the inner thoughts and feelings of everyone. Once she discerns the intents of their hearts, she humbly falls to her knees to intercede on their behalves then jubilantly springs to her feet to share herself with them. She often would provide motivating signs of the requested answer as shared with her by God. She encourages them, insisting that they remain expectant, confident and resolute.

Hope likes to foster a sense of optimistic expectancy. She is a relentless optimist always believing for the best in everyone and that the best will come out of every situation! She is not distracted or dismayed by potential or realized roadblocks that stand in the path to her goals. She always sees the silver lining and encourages you to see it with her.

When others speak about Hope they say that she inspires them, encourages them. She holds up their hands when they get too tired and has their backs when situations take a turn for the worse. Hope stands ready and able at your back, opened palm, pushing you to keep moving when your legs are too tired to take even one more step forward. Hope models how to keep your head held high in the face of certain despair, turmoil, or rejection. Hope insists on being hopeful and her aptitude of hope determines both her attitude and altitude.

Hope feels hopeful about you, about your future, your desires, your wants, your children, your relationships, your career, your finances, your today and tomorrow, your everything. Hope embodies Jeremiah 29 v.11 as she believes that God knows the plans He has for her, plans to prosper her, and not to harm her, plans to give her hope and a future.

Because of Hope:

One becomes **hopeful** when they befriend Hope. Hope breeds hope. One's heart fills with expectation when they befriend Hope. There is an expectation for progress, success, healing, financial breakthrough, protection for your children, and God's favor. Expectation wells up to become a flood of trust. It becomes a stalwart trust in the fact that the boundless hope would eventually become a reality in time. One becomes full of hope, so that there is no space or crevice left for doubt, or distrust. Our body, our affect, our heart exudes hope that would ensure that your thoughts and your actions are fastened with the anchors of trust, faith and prayer.

Hope is unaffected by the passage of time, instead as time passes, hope multiplies, replicates, breeds hope and maintains a steady, sure and resolute belief that hope will one day, in time, be rewarded. Hope values the passage of time as the opportunity for due season and due reward to coincide. Not that Hope believes there to be a coincidental occurrence in answer to her hope. In stark contrast, Hope believes there to be a planned, predestined, chosen point in time that the desires of her heart will be granted. Her joy in hope, though seemingly delayed, is that in due season she will receive her due reward in and for her hope.

Hope makes you **harmonious** with all you meet, everyone you engage with, those you encounter, those who mean you harm, those who plot and conspire against you, with defeat, failure, with loss. Hope makes you harmonious. Hope, being laser-focused on the desires of her heart; is not willing to stray from the path of harmony that will lead her to her goal. So she will not allow anything or anyone to distract her, to her detriment, from her reward for which she hopes.

Hope then must live every day in harmony with others, with herself, and with her God. She will not reap the harvest of her hope without this consistent, daily harmonious realignment. Her 'struggle' then becomes to remain in a state of harmony which is the vehicle for her journey to the reward for her hope.

I Thessalonians 4 v. 13-18

13 Brothers and sisters, we do not want you to be uninformed about those who sleep in death, so that you do not grieve like the rest of mankind, who have no hope. **14** For we believe that Jesus died and rose again, and so we believe that God will bring with Jesus those who have fallen asleep in him. **15** According to the Lord's word, we tell you that we who are still alive, who are left until the coming of the Lord, will certainly not precede those who have fallen asleep. **16** For the Lord himself will come down from heaven, with a loud command, with the voice of the archangel and with the trumpet call of God, and the dead in Christ will rise first. **17** After that, we who are still alive and are left will be caught up together with them in the clouds to meet the Lord in the air. And so we will be with the Lord forever. **18** Therefore encourage one another with these words.

Hope's global positioning device is always set to home. Hope makes you **heavenly focused** as her primary goal is to get to heaven. Her hope is to be with the Lord, whether she dies before His second coming or whether she is on the earth when He returns. With this being her steadfast hope, Hope is able to buoy you through life's challenges and disappointments up to and past death. Hope's hope is eternal.

As a friend:

Hope along with Charity and Faith cheers for you all day and night. Hope has the ideas of what you can and will become and devotes her time and energy working to make sure you get there. She is always concerned about how you are doing, how life is treating you, how things are going for you and how she can make things better. She listens to everything you do and do not say. She listens to your heart, captures it's sentiment and then sets about to give you the desires of which she learned.

Hope is the friend that is excited and supportive about any and all of your hair brained ideas; backs you fully regarding them and leaves you more hopeful than before you shared the idea with her.

Hope is your prayer warrior friend. She consistently stands in the gap for you interceding on your behalf. She understands the desire of her girlfriends' hearts and then intercedes on their behalves. Hope is always in your corner, hoping for the best for you, and everything about you.

She is an independent thinker, cares little about what others think about her, neither is moved by others' opinions of her. Hope is not haughty or arrogant, instead she is humbled by the potential impossibility of her requests yet remains full of confident expectation.

Girlfriend to Girlfriend:

- Hang in there! God knows where you are.
- Befriend me when it seems it is useless to do so.
- Remember to pray for what you hope for.
- Understand that Faith and I should always be friends.
- Try to share me with someone else, for so many lack hope.

Hope in Quotation Marks:

"Sanguine expectation for something to occur."

Her Hashtags:

#confidentexpectation
#wanttobetrue
#nodoubt
#shamelesswants
#inthegap
#hopejoy

<u>Your Turn</u>

_____
_____
_____

Recognizing Hope:
- Seeing the bright side of things.
- Recognizing that a rainbow comes after the rain.
- Recognizing that joy comes in the morning.
- Remaining optimistic in the face of adversity.
- Optimism
- Praying without ceasing.
- Expecting miracles.

<u>Your Turn</u>

- _____
- _____
- _____

Acknowledgement:

Whenever I am down about anything, I message my friend Hope. It is she that cheers me up, makes me feel better about whatever is going on and insists that I see the greener side of things. Hope gives me hope!

Reflection on Hope:

1. Your thoughts to or about Hope -

   _____
   _____
   _____
   _____
   _____

2. How does Hannah's hope resonate with you?

   _____
   _____
   _____
   _____
   _____

3. Is it possible for life's experiences to render one hopeless instead of hopeful? How so?

   _____
   _____
   _____
   _____

4. As humans, what or whom do we often have hope in? In whom should we have our hope and why?

   _____
   _____

5. What would be the difference, if any, as you see it, between hope and ambition? Which one did Tamar have? Which one was rewarded? Justify your answer.

6. If you had to symbolize hope with an inanimate object. What would it be and why?

7. Recall or write a song, poem or jingle to remind you of your friend, Hope.

8. Is there a difference between the girlfriends, Hope and Faith?

Assignment:
1. Start writing the book; recording your poems, painting your picture, or penning the lines to a song; believe!
2. Fulfill someone's hope; donate, share, give, serve.
3. Show your children the connection between their hopes and what happens in their lives.
4. Complete the application for the new job or degree.
5. Ask for the raise.
6. Try out for the team, audition for the play.
7. After prayer, ask for his hand in marriage.
8. Wake, expecting your dreams to come true.
9. Read your Bible asking God to show you something in his word to renew your hope.
10. Pray for God's will. Pray that God grant you your desires and hopes according to his will.

Girlfriend Favor

un**F**air

Approving

pri**V**ilege

Opportunistic

p**R**eferential

Favor

Definition: approval, acceptance; special benefits or blessings.

Origin: Middle English

Meaning: Approval

Bible Verses:
Psalms 5:12 - For thou, LORD, wilt bless the righteous; with favor wilt thou compass him as [with] a shield.

Psalm 30:5 "For his anger is but for a moment, and his favor is for a lifetime. Weeping may tarry for the night, but joy comes with the morning."

Psalm 84:11 "For the Lord God is a sun and shield; the Lord bestows favor and honor. No good thing does he withhold from those who walk uprightly."

Bible Reference:
Esther 2 v 17

Queen Esther's story is saturated with favor. She was an orphan adopted by her uncle, then later presented herself to the king, Xerxes. Xerxes was the king who had a wife in which he was displeased. In time, the king showered Esther with favor and made her his queen. Queen Esther went from the orphanage to the the throne.

Women of Favor in the Bible:
- *Bathsheba* - She bore King David a son out of an adulterous relationship as she was the wife of Uriah; whom David had killed. The child died but God granted David and Bathsheba favor with another famed son, King Solomon, meaning "Beloved of the Lord."
- *Elisabeth* - Though she was married for many years to Zacharias, they had no children. Elisabeth remained patient and waited on the Lord. In her old age, God favored Elisabeth and gave her John. Elisabeth was also favored in that she was the first woman to confess Jesus in the flesh.
- *Elisheba* became the female founder of the Levitical priesthood. (Exodus 6 v 23)

- *Esther* obtained grace and favor in the King's eyes instead of Queen Vashti. (The Book of Esther)
- *Hagar* ill-treated by Sarah, her owner, bade God's command to return to her. Upon her obedience, God made a promise that her son would be a father to a great multitude.
- *Hannah,* the favored wife of Elkanah could not bare children, suffered at the tongue of Elkanah's second wife and was after prayer and supplication granted favor and was given Samuel.
- *Mary,* the mother of Jesus, is highly revered over all women. The Bible says she was highly favored and found favor in God. This, I believe is an understatement as she was chosen to bear the Christ child! (Luke 1:28, 30)
- *Ruth,* daugher in law to a widowed and aging Naomi, sought work in order to provide for herself and Naomi upon their return to Jerusalem. She gained the favor and the hand of an aging Boaz thereby rising from poverty to plenty. By their union and child, she also became an ancestress of the Christ King. (The Book of Ruth)
- *Sarah* was 90 years old when she conceived a son to her long wedded husband, Abraham. Abraham was favored by God to be the patriarchs of many nations. (Genesis 17 and 18)

About Favor:

Favor shows kindness beyond what is due. This is relatively ironic, because the human race is sinful and not due God's kindness. In response to our sin, our unkindness, God provides Favor. She spends time thinking about ways that she can show you God's favor. Favor has noted countless ways; a short list includes - giving you a restful night sleep, providing you shelter, waking you up each morning, providing food for your bodies, giving you a car to drive, gas to put in it, somewhere to go to earn money, etc.

Favor approves of you. Despite all of your issues, drama, sin, dispositions, selfishness, idiosyncrasies, God and Favor still approve and accept you. For they see what you would be without them as well as what you can be because of them. They recognize that you need them in your life and that their favor needs to be granted to you each day.

Everyone loves Favor! They aim to gain approval from Favor. They want Favor to like them. They know that Favor dispenses welcomed kindness as needed and is incapable of doing them harm; so everyone aims to please and remain in good graces with Favor.

Because of Favor:

Being **favored** is a direct result of God's favor. When God favors you, you experience benefits; from your ability to rise each day, to protection as you travel, to sustenance and providence, to the attainment of a good night's sleep, to these and many more benefits being extended to you and yours daily. When you are friends with Favor, you benefit from her in pronounced ways like getting the job for which you were not as qualified for, or gaining the scholarship despite an enormous number of other suitably qualified applicants. Favor extends herself to you in less pronounced ways as well; like allowing you the opportunity to arrive just in time to get the last of your favorite muffins at the bakery or having you to be chosen for a small incentive on your job.

Fearless is how one can be described when they are favored with favor. There is a boldness, a confidence that one wears like a badge of honor when one is fearless. They are fearless, for they know that favor is a hedge of protection around them covering the hairs on their head all the way down to their very toes. There is a fearless, unbounded demeanor assumed when one see no limits, and recognizes that favor is a hedge as well as a safety net. With this being the case, there is no need to fear anything; sickness, loss, tragedy, trauma; nothing. Someone who intimately knows Favor is fearless and lives their lives understanding that they are saturated with and by Favor and therefore have nothing to fear. Favor is grounded in Second Timothy Chapter 1 verse 7, we are reminded, 'For God has not given us a spirit of fear, but of power and of love and of a sound mind.'

Because of Favor we are **free.** We are free to live life to the fullest, confident that our hedge and safety net of favor are firmly in place. We are free to believe that our hopes, our desires, our ideas can come to fruition. We are free to help and support others with the understanding that favor will replenish our needs, compensate for our deficits. We are free to apply for the job that we want, though some may believe it is out of our reach. We are free to believe in a God from whom comes all of our help, and who penned an enduring assurance in my favorite verse in the Bible; Jeremiah 29 verse 11 'For I know the plans I have for you," declares the Lord, "plans to prosper you and not to harm you, plans to give you hope and a future.' - FAVOR!

As a friend:

Favor is an equal-opportunity friend. She does not discriminate regarding who can be her friend, she is friend to anyone despite who they are, who they will become, their language, intellect, desires, futures, etc. Favor loves to be a friend, in the truest sense of the word.

Favor spoils everyone she knows, especially her girlfriends! She is the one that will cover the bill on a girl's night out, shower you with gifts at your bridal or baby shower, take you on a shopping trip, spend countless hours with you even when she would rather be somewhere else, help you write a soon to be due paper, and repeat her counsel even though it has been ignored time and time again. Favor chooses to hang out with you, cater to your needs, and fix things for you so you don't have to.

Favor is the friend that picks up the dress, shoe or purse for you while shopping for herself at the mall; not because you asked for it, but just because it looked like you and she thought you might like it!

Favor increases, to a great degree, the level of happiness in each friend's heart. Favor knows how to make things even better than they are. Favor brings goodness, exceeds contentment, makes you smile, and makes you awesomely happy!

Girlfriend to Girlfriend:
- When I bless you, bless someone else.
- Remember that I share myself with everyone and there always is enough of me to go around.
- You are to claim me as friend.
- As you can never repay me, you must commit to share the bounty of my favor with someone else.

Favor in Quotation Marks:

"Approval with benefits."

Her Hashtags:

#onlyforsome
#fringebenefits
#countlessblessings
#foralifetime
#asashield

<u>Your Turn</u>

_____
_____
_____

Recognizing Favor:
- Getting a job.
- Getting the job you didn't deserve.
- Having good health.
- Surviving an accident.
- Getting a promotion.
- Having job satisfaction.
- Buying a house.
- Earning a degree.
- Having your needs met.
- Having your wants met.

<u>Your Turn</u>
- _____
- _____
- _____

Acknowledgement:
Everyone needs a friend like Favor! I thank God for Favor every day. I can see Favor show up and show out in my life in every instance and/or circumstance. Favor is especially kind and gracious to those she loves and truth be told, she loves her girlfriends!

Reflection on Favor:

1. Your thoughts to or about Favor -

   _____
   _____
   _____
   _____
   _____

2. Which of the Bible verses highlighted above about Favor gives you the greatest sense of safety, protection or providence?

   _____

3. We've all heard, Favor is not fair. Which of the women of Favor do you believe was the most favored and why?

4. How can we attain more of God's Favor?

5. How can you tell if you are out of God's favor?

6. Why might God delay dispensing His favor in our lives?

7. I have always said if I were to get a personalized license plate, It would either read, 'Favor' or 'Favored' or some other version to celebrate God's favor on and over my life as well as being besties with Favor. Would we have matching license plates, or which girlfriend might you choose for your license plate?

_____
_____
_____
_____

Assignment:
1. Shower someone with unexpected gifts.
2. Tell someone you appreciate them.
3. Publicly approve someone's work, effort, success, etc.
4. Give to someone; money, clothing, time, effort.
5. Claim favor and do something that you'd prayed about and wanted to do.
6. Thank God for the favor He's shown you.
7. Pray that God's favor be granted to others as it was granted to you.

Girlfriend Serenity

Seeks peace

shuns strifE

gRacious

Even-keeled

harmoNious

freeIng

perfecT

imperturbabilitY

Serenity

Definition: freedom from disturbance; the state of mental calm, peaceful; harmonious living with others.

Origin: Middle English

Meaning: Peaceful

Bible Verses:
Philippians 4 v 7
And the peace of God, which passeth all understanding, shall keep your hearts and minds through Christ Jesus.

Proverbs 16 v 7
When a man's ways please the Lord, he maketh even his enemies to be at peace with him.

Isaiah 26 v 3
Thou wilt keep him in perfect peace, whose mind is stayed on thee: because he trusteth in thee.

Psalms 34 v 14
Depart from evil, and do good; seek peace, and pursue it.

Bible Reference:
John 19

When Jesus stood before Pilate in perfect peace; it confounded and infuriated Pilate. Jesus was facing certain death amid taunts, cries for his crucifixion, humiliation, and unjust rage. Yet, he stood before Pilate in perfect peace, answering his questions with righteous indignation and an indescribable peace that could not be understood.

Women of Serenity in the Bible:
- Hannah, the favored wife of Elkanah could not bare children, suffered peaceably at the tongue of Elkanah's second wife and was after prayer and supplication granted mercy and favor and was given Samuel.

- *Noah's wife* had peace along with her husband that confounded others as he endured ridicule as he built an ark by God's command for the impending and promised flood. (Genesis 6:18; 7:1, 7, 13; 8:16, 18)
- Rahab, hid the men of God with an assured peace that she was doing the right thing and that her faith would be rewarded and that she would be spared from certain destruction. (Joshua 2:1, 3; 6:17-25)
- Queen *Vashti,* a chaste and modest feminist peacefully, adamantly and at great cost refused the command of her drunk husband to be his call-girl at a feast. Her refusal to degrade herself; disobey the law and customs, and fulfill the lust of her kingly husband and his other guests was severely punished as she was denounced as queen and lost her empire and its associated luxuries. (Esther 1; 2:1; 4:17)

About Serenity:

Serenity is difficult to describe primarily because what she allows us to experience, through the power of God, confounds our understanding. When there is a state of true, God-given peace, the human mind cannot comprehend it. It is beyond our capacity to understand how God ordered everything, changed hearts, moved persons out of the way and set things in order just in time to grant you His peace.

Serenity is a personal state of being; experienced only by you. Therefore she cannot be shared in her entirety; though some of her resultant characteristics can certainly be shared. For example, Serenity may share a smile with you though you would expect her to frown due to her circumstances. She may seem oblivious to the negative situation that is starkly obvious to everyone else. She may like Jesus walk confidently and unaffected down a path to her certain demise; though everyone around us, much like the crowd surrounding Jesus, taunts her or holds their breath hoping that she turn around thereby shunning her fate.

Serenity has feelings of peace toward us. She is unaffected by all the ills, evil, and sin that seeks to consume us. She instead, confounds our understanding, and walks through the very valley of death with peace, being in harmony with God and man. This shows her unfailing trust for and in God, and her confidence that His word will not return to Him void.

With this confidence, Serenity never experiences the feelings of doubt, apprehension, fear, or disharmony. In contrast, God enables Serenity to create an atmosphere of love, acceptance, grace, mercy, hope, favor, trust, and faith that is best felt and experienced though difficult to put in words or be understood.

Because of Serenity:

Serenity allows you to be **satisfied**. This fulfilling and joyous sense of satisfaction is afforded when one experiences true serenity; true calm and true bliss. For joy is a direct result of serenity. There is a sweet, insatiable and penetrating joy that is immediately evident in everything we do, to and with everyone we meet. It is highly enveloping to those whom we encounter. Serenity evokes feelings of this joyous nature, because though there may be conflict, contention, strife, struggle, problems, despair, loss, and or death; in the midst of any and all of that, there exists in your heart and mind a sense of tranquility, satisfaction, hope, faith, trust and an impregnable conviction that no harm will come to you that God himself has not tempered with His mercy. This serenity is unexplainable; it truly does, pass ALL understanding as asserted and assured us in Philippians 4 v. 7; And the peace of God, which surpasses all understanding, will guard your hearts and your minds in Christ Jesus.

While one is in a state of serenity; they feel **sheltered,** protected, safe and secure. Serenity insulates your mind and heart, though your body may still be affected. It grants you an inward peace and solace that grants you shelter in the midst of any storm. This shelter affords you the blessed assurance of Psalm 46.

Psalm 46 King James Version (KJV)

1 God is our refuge and strength, a very present help in trouble.

2 Therefore will we not fear, though the earth be removed, and though the mountains be carried into the midst of the sea;

3 Though the waters thereof roar and be troubled, though the mountains shake with the swelling thereof. Selah.

4 There is a river, the streams whereof shall make glad the city of God, the holy place of the tabernacles of the most High.

5 God is in the midst of her; she shall not be moved: God shall help her, and that right early.

6 The heathen raged, the kingdoms were moved: he uttered his voice, the earth melted.

7 The Lord of hosts is with us; the God of Jacob is our refuge. Selah.

8 Come, behold the works of the Lord, what desolations he hath made in the earth.

9 He maketh wars to cease unto the end of the earth; he breaketh the bow, and cutteth the spear in sunder; he burneth the chariot in the fire.

10 Be still, and know that I am God: I will be exalted among the heathen, I will be exalted in the earth.

11 The Lord of hosts is with us; the God of Jacob is our refuge. Selah.

Serenity is **satiable** and **sustainable**. A sense of serenity keeps you going, gives you inspiration, fuel, power, strength and drive when it seems to others and even yourself, at times, that all hope may be lost and that there is no way out that you can perceive. Upon the acknowledgement that you cannot deliver yourself, see the future, nor see the way out of no way, you tap your reserve tank of serenity. You relax, you become still and in that stillness you become acutely aware that God is… a shelter, a comfort, the answer, the hope, the peace, … God, all by himself. He does not need us. He sustains.

As a friend:

Serenity is the calm friend. Consequently, she never gets ruffled, anxious, frustrated or angry. She scampers away, in the opposite direction, from any type of controversy or strife. She keeps all of her other friends centered and appeased.

Serenity is also unsuspectingly powerful. When she enters a room, she quiets it in one fell swoop as discord, dissention or friction can no longer occupy the space when Serenity enters.

Serenity is the girlfriend that is hardest to describe. Her friendship is best when experienced. She confounds even her friends with her ability to keep her calm even when her world is in disarray, things aren't going like they should or the way she wants them to. She is the friend that when her husband walks out on her with five young children, she still finds the wherewithal to greet everyone with a smile, be cordial to him when he decides to call, and refrain from transferring her feelings about him to the children.

Serenity possesses the ability to treat everyone with respect and regard even after being passed over for the promotion time and time again. She would still, despite the obvious and repeated slight, show up to work on time every day, give her best effort, and smile though underappreciated and underpaid.

Girlfriend to Girlfriend:
- Your level of contentment and sense of purpose greatly increases as you get to know me better.
- If you ever feel like I am not with you when making a decision, you should either refrain from making the decision or postpone it.
- I am the friend closest to you when you do what is right.
- Befriend me, as our friendship will lead to Joy.

Serenity in Quotation Marks:

"Calm waters despite the struggle beneath."

Her Hashtags:

#perfectpeace
#passesallunderstanding
#peaceinthestorm
#unshaken
#serenitythroughthestruggle
#undisturbed
#placid

Your Turn
_____
_____
_____

Recognizing Serenity:
- Being gracious to those who are less than gracious to you.
- Smiling while in the storms of life.
- Keeping your cool when it is more logical to be enraged.
- Not retaliating despite the circumstance.

<u>Your Turn</u>
- _____
- _____
- _____

Acknowledgement:

    I love Serenity because she keeps me aware of the peace that comes from God. She provides a peace that only He can give and that even my enemies cannot take away. I begin my day with Serenity, bid her to stay with me all day and thank her for staying with me through the night.

Reflection on Serenity:

1. Your thoughts to or about Serenity -

   _____
   _____
   _____
   _____
   _____

2. How could we live the premises of Psalm 34 v 14?

   _____
   _____
   _____
   _____

3. I have always appreciated the story of Queen Esther for her faith, loyalty and courage. However, Queen Vashti's story, without which there would not be a Queen Esther story, has become one of my favorite about Serenity. What does her story mean to you?

   _____
   _____

4. If you had to name antagonists to Serenity; what would they be?

8. Why is Serenity so elusive?

5. Relate a time when you had a sense of serenity about something in your life that no one including you could understand?

Assignment:
1. Pray for God's peace in your life and in the lives of those you love.
2. Take a peaceful walk.
3. Watch a 'feel good' movie.
4. Read the Bible asking and expecting God to show you something in His word to grant you peace.
5. Listen to peaceful, relaxing music or the ebb and flow of the ocean's waves.
6. Take an exercise or yoga class.
7. Read a book.
8. Place your trust in the Lord.
9. Take solace in your decision that you made as a result of prayer.
10. Avoid contentious conversation.

Girlfriend Honesty

Honorable

mOral

kiNd

objectivE

tranSparent

imparTial

veritY

Honesty

Definition: fairness, straightforward conduct

Origin: English

Meaning: Truthfulness

Bible Verses:
Ephesians 4 v 25
Wherefore putting away lying, speak every man truth with his neighbour: for we are members one of another.

Luke 6 v 31
And as ye would that men should do to you, do ye also to them likewise.

Proverbs 12 v 22
Lying lips are an abomination to the Lord: but they that deal truly are his delight.

Bible Reference:
Acts 5 v 11

Ananias and Sapphira, husband and wife, told a lie to God. They were a well-to-do couple who were able to sell a possession. They were to bring the full sale price to the prophet; instead greed grabbed them. They kept back part of the profit and insisted that they'd brought the full sum to the prophet. God showed them the error of their way, took Ananias' life and three hours later took the life of Sapphira.

Women of Honesty in the Bible:

- *Deborah* - a prophetess and a judge - she had the gift of discernment, was spoken to and through by God. She dispensed judgments of grace and mercy sitting under a tree bearing her name. She was also a warrior and gained fame by defeating her enemies and rescuing her people.
- *Hagar* - though wronged by Sarah honored the arrangement she had with her family and returned to her service at God's counsel. (Genesis 16; 21:9-17; 25:12; Galatians 4:24, 25)

- *Harlot mother, (there were two),* would rather live without her child than have him severed because of the untrue word of her callous companion spoken before King Solomon who claimed the remaining living child was hers. (1 Kings 3)
- *Huldah* was in harmony with God and was consulted when the lost book of the law was found. Huldah's prophetic message and the reading of the law brought about a revival in the land.
- *Lydia,* an astute business woman, as she was well-known for her sale of purple dye sought God daily for grace and knowledge to run her business. She, upon her conversion, told others in her household who were likewise converted and baptized. (Acts 16 v 14)

About Honesty:

Honesty is a burden bearer as her burden is all that makes up moral character; integrity, truthfulness, straightforwardness, loyalty, fairness, sincerity, empathy, courage, and fortitude. Though her burden is great, Honesty does not tire as she undergirds each of these heavy, necessary and important virtues. She instead remains unmoved and insistent that the values of her virtue can lead, guide, sustain and support the values of all other virtues. For without honesty, there is no other moral character or virtue. Each of the others require the guidelines and attributes that Honesty testifies of.

Honesty knows everything about you. Despite your secret thoughts and feelings that are in direct opposition to the very fiber of Honesty; she loves you. She only has and fosters thoughts and feelings toward you that will show you her love. Consequently, Honesty's actions demonstrate God's love.

Others often have varied feelings toward Honesty, though hers never change. They sometimes have feelings of appreciation for Honesty because she speaks in their favor and to their benefit. At other times, many feel disdain for Honesty because she speaks against their heart's desires, intents or inclinations.

Honesty likes to expose truth; however condemning, revealing, shame causing, or detrimental it may be. Honesty chooses truth regardless of the consequence every time. She realizes that God delights in those who deal honestly with everyone and in every situation. She exists to have God delight!

Because of Honesty:

Because of Honesty, you will be **honest.** You will honor your word, you will speak only what you know you can do and commit to only what you are capable of following through with. You will be honest with all you encounter even when it is unpopular to be so, or when it is easier to be deceitful. You will not suffer from having a twin-tongue; you will say only what you mean and you will mean what you say. You will expect that others are honest as well. You will find it incredulous that anyone would be dishonest especially because you are fully aware, whether by experience or education that the truth will find you out. You then see the exercise of dishonesty to be vain, nonsense and time consuming. You know that honesty will always expose you, your actions, and your deceit. So you choose to be honest, because of Honesty.

As truth always trumps a lie; Honesty makes you **humble**. Honesty forces you to recognize that there is a higher power, far higher than yourself. Honesty humbles you, not in a shaming sense of the word, as that is the preference of dishonesty. Honesty makes you humble, aware, modest, chaste, and God-fearing. It is impossible, without humility, to boldly tell the truth regardless of the consequences, to throw yourself under the x-ray vision of honesty without first humbling yourself with the help of Honesty.

Honesty makes you **honorable**. The dispositions of Honesty and Honor are interchangeable. It is impossible to be honorable without honesty and likewise it is impossible to be honest and not be considered honorable. The beauty of honesty and honor is that there is no change needed in order to be considered both, for an honest act is an honorable act. One may gain public honor because of their honesty, but whether the honor is bestowed publicly or not, the honor is germane to being honest.

There is a certain public stature that comes when one is honest. For society will look up to you more, they will ensure that others know you to be honest regarded, reputable and honored. This pedestal may be shoved under your feet because of your acts of honesty by others who regard your actions, but an honest heart cannot be given or taken by men.

As a friend:

If you want a straight answer, Honesty is the friend you need. She has the uncanny ability to tell you like it is, straighten you out, and serve you up the truth all with a dose of love, affection, kindness and candor.

Honesty is the friend that everyone is careful not to question or challenge unless they are prepared for the answer. Preparation for the answer that Honesty provides requires a mental adjustment; for one has to settle in their mind that they are willing to accept the answer; willing to handle the truth. As Honesty does not lie, when a girlfriend asks about her weight, her hair, her makeup, her boyfriend, her cleanliness, her culinary skill or lack of; she has to be prepared for and willing to accept the answer.

Honesty does not show favoritism; everyone gets the same treatment, the same blunt and matter of fact response. Honesty is not going to have anyone in the girlfriend group believe her to be dishonest, partial or shady. Honesty insists that everyone knows her to be as her name declares she is.

Honesty will always seek the truth, prefer it, and preach it. In financial dealings, she is the auditor. In matters of the heart, she is sensitive and fair. Regarding family matters, she is impartial, kind and seeks to maintain the familial bonds. In matters of arbitration, she exposes the shortcomings, the misgivings and the failures of those opposed to her virtue.

In all she does, Honesty lives up to her name.

Girlfriend to Girlfriend:
- Be honest with yourself at all times and in every situation.
- Insist that others are always honest with you.
- Be honest in all your dealings.
- Be willing to accept and benefit from other's honesty with and regarding you.

Honesty in Quotation Marks:

"The undergirding virtue of moral character."

Her Hashtags:

#truth
#asitis
#impartial
#Hisdelight

Your Turn

\# _____
\# _____
\# _____

Recognizing Honesty:
- Accepting the foul when playing a game.
- Following the rules when no one appears to be looking.
- Giving your testimony even though it is painful.
- Telling the truth when stopped for a speeding ticket.
- Owning it and apologizing when you've done wrong.
- Sharing your innermost feelings with God.
- Arriving on time for work and working diligently all day and remaining until quitting time.
- Telling the truth regardless of the consequences.

<u>Your Turn</u>
- _____
- _____
- _____

Acknowledgement:
 Honesty is one of the friends whose attributes I most aim to possess. I must be honest and show integrity in all my dealings with everyone regardless of the imminent consequences, be they fair or foul.

Reflection on Honesty:
1. Your thoughts to or about Honesty -

   _____
   _____
   _____
   _____
   _____

2. Identify which of the verses noted above you wished everyone in your relationships knew and followed. Why so?

   _____
   _____
   _____
   _____
   _____

3. Many of the women in the Bible gained favor, grace and/or privilege due to acts of deceit. Why do you think that is? How does this counter with the phrase, "by any means necessary?"

   _____
   _____
   _____
   _____

4. Honesty plays a part in everything we do, say, feel, think, or share. Do you agree with that claim?

5. Defend, whether there would be a 'moral code' without honesty?

6. Pick a public forum; politics, pastorship, teacher, business woman, etc. Is practicing honesty difficult in these arenas? Why or why not?

7. What are the sins in your life that dishonesty has laid the foundation for?

8. There are very few women named as women of honesty in the Bible? Why do you think that may be? Who, from the Bible, would you add to the list?

_____

_____

_____

_____

_____

Assignment:
1. Tell the truth.
2. Deal honestly with everyone.

Girlfriend Harmony

togetHer

Aligned

agReeable

like-Minded

Orderly

in syNc

unifYing

Harmony

Definition: accord, consistent, orderly and pleasing arrangement of parts.

Origin: Greek

Meaning: A beautiful blending

Bible Verses:
Amos 3 v 3
Can two walk together, except they be agreed?

Psalm 133 v 1
Behold, how good and how pleasant it is for brethren to dwell together in unity!

Romans 12 v 16
Be of the same mind one toward another. Mind not high things, but condescend to men of low estate. Be not wise in your own conceits.

Bible Reference:
Acts 1 12-14
The Upper Room Prayer Meeting is the most powerful story demonstrating harmony in the Bible that I could find. In the Upper Room, harmony was pervasive as all that were in the room, men and women, rich and poor, humble or haughty, weak or strong alike were in one accord in prayer and supplication.

Women of Harmony in the Bible:
- *Elisabeth* - a righteous woman and along with her husband, Zacharias, walked in all the commandments of the Lord.
- *Eve* - in total harmony with her husband, Adam after she was created out of his rib. Sadly, they were also in harmony to disobey the commandment of God and eat of the tree of good and evil.
- *Sarah* gave Hagar to Abraham against the will and promises of God; Abraham and Sarah were in harmony to sin against God.
- *Huldah* was in harmony with God and was consulted when the lost book of the law was found. Huldah's prophetic message and the reading of the law brought about a revival in the land.

- *Naomi and Ruth,* mother and daughter in law remained together in harmony after becoming widowed, returned to Bethlehem from Moab, assisted each other and were able to live comfortably after Ruth and Boaz are wed. (The Book of Ruth)
- *Priscilla* and her husband Aquila harmoniously worked in the service of the Lord, in their family tent-making business. They had love and affection for the Apostle Paul, knew the scriptures and laid down their lives in harmonic martyrdom.
- *Puah and Shiprah*, two Egyptian midwives who were in charge of a large number of midwives directed to kill the Israelite males upon their births. The women together determined that true to their faith they could not do such and claimed that the babies were born they could get to them, thereby sparing their lives. (Exodus 15 v. 1-21).
- *Salome* and Zebedee were the parents of James and John, two beloved disciples of Jesus. As parents, they harmoniously reared their children in the fear and admonition of the Lord and were honored by their children's service to God. (Matthew 20:20-24; 27:56; Mark 10:35-40; 15:40, 41; 16:1, 2)
- *Sapphira,* wife of Ananias, enjoyed a harmonious relationship with each other. Both converted from Judaism to Christianity. Many christians upon conversion sold their belongings and put the money in a common fund for the good of all believers. They were in harmony to lie to God claiming that they had sold the property and given all the money to God. (Acts 5 vs. 1-11)
- *Wise Hearted women*, served the church by joyfully, willingly and without reward hand-making woven cloths for the completion of the Tabernacle of the Lord. (Exodus 35 vs 22-29)
- *Woman of Shunem,* in harmony with her husband, provided her home and the apartment she built for him as a dwelling for Elisha as he traveled telling of Christ.

About Harmony:

Harmony aims to have her feelings, thoughts, emotions and heart's desires to be transferred to you. She stays close to you, seeks an intimate relationship with you for this reason. She wants everything within her to be a part of your existence. She knows that in order for her to be intimate with you, she has to get you to emulate her thoughts, desires, emotions, etc. Harmony does not wish for you to pattern your life after her because of her pride or self-conception. She wishes for you pattern your life after her because she knows that she is the path to intimacy with Serenity, which she desperately desires for you.

Harmony seeks a symbiotic relationship with you. She knows that such a relationship will bring mutual benefit to both parties. She knows that accord, order and symbiosis helps to shape your purpose, your potential, your promise and your product.

She knows that neither of those will be realized if you are not in a relationship of Harmony with your God, yourself, your spouse, your family, your friends, etc. Therefore her life's mission is to get you to Harmony.

When Harmony is described, she is often described as intuitive, instinctive, like-minded and organized. Harmony is described in these ways because she 'reads you', judges the distance of your thoughts, actions and feelings from harmony and works to bridge the distance. She can't do her work in confusion, instead she is organized, thoughtful and strategically planned in order to bring your thoughts into accordance with her own.

Because of Harmony:

Harmony makes you **happy**! When everything is as it should be, the way you like it, peaceful, settled; you will become happy. This happiness is unique for there may not be visible and evident signs to others of your state of harmony. This happiness, may be born out of a harmonized satisfaction that only you can experience, sense, feel or may have. A sense of harmony, does not however mean that you won't ever feel sad, dejected, etc; it simply means that because your life is in harmony with God, you have an unceasing joy, happiness, hope, that come ebb or flow of life, you remain with Harmony.

A **hospitable** disposition is a natural result of being in harmony. You will as a result of your desired state of harmony, want to share with others. You will want to share your happiness, your hope, your dinner table, your unused clothing, your extra and at times, even when you lack material possessions; you will want to share your God. A sense of harmony allows you to recognize that though you experience seasons of plenty and seasons of need, you are the daughter of a King, The Heavenly Father and an omnipotent Jehovah Jireh. He will replenish what you give in service to others and in obedience to Him.

When you are in a state of harmony, you become more and more **humane**. Not human, as that is already the case, but you become more humane. You become more likely to show benevolence or compassion. As you experience a state of harmony, you want others to experience the same, you strive to have them to experience what you have. What you have, may not be at all tangible or materialistic, instead, it may be things like time, love, compassion, hope, faith, etc. This quest to try to meet the needs of others, regardless of what it is, how much it may cost you, or where it may be found, is what harmony prods you to do as you become more and more humane.

As a friend:

Harmony recognizes each girlfriend for their uniqueness in addition to how their uniqueness contributes to the completeness of the whole group. Harmony understands that in order for each girlfriend to get what they need from the relationships with each other they need to be allowed the opportunity to be themselves.

Harmony believes in order, not in a hierarchical sense as she ensures that no friend assumes that they are better than the other. She instead will stoop to reach those that are in need of her. She believes in the order that exists within the boundaries of friendship. She insists that each friend be true to their role, make their contribution and do so consistently in a manner that does not brew discord, dissent, dissatisfaction or ill-willed competition within the group.

Harmony understands that friendship is an endless ebb and flow. Her role within the group is to maintain the ebb and flow that naturally exists; the ups, the downs, the problems, the successes, the heartache, the pain, the joy, and the hope. Harmony works incessantly to maintain, in essence, the balance of friendship, our relationships and our lives.

Girlfriend to Girlfriend:

- Work towards me.
- Do everything in an orderly manner.
- Seek persons who also recognize the benefits of me.
- Do everything in balance.

Harmony in Quotation Marks:

"Symbiosis of the mind, heart, soul and body."

Her Hashtags:

#giveandtake
#inone
#walktogether
#agreed
#unified
#insync

<u>Your Turn</u>

\# _____

\# _____

\# _____

Recognizing Harmony:
- Getting along with everyone
- Nature
- Intimate relationships
- Familial relationships

<u>Your Turn</u>

- _____
- _____
- _____

Acknowledgement:

Girlfriends often have so much baggage, so much that they bring to the table; to the friendship. It is therefore imperative that every group of girlfriends includes Harmony. It is only she that can successfully navigate the waters of female friendships as those waters often require the benefits only Harmony provides.

Reflection on Harmony:

1. Your thoughts to or about Harmony -

   _____
   _____
   _____
   _____
   _____

2. Taking a look at the 'Women of Harmony', which of the women do you feel demonstrated harmony the way that you either currently are or the way you want to in your life?

   _____

3. Do you feel that Harmony is dependent on Honesty? Could one have harmony without honesty?

4. Harmony dictates the success or failure of every relationship. Do you agree or disagree?

Assignment:
1. Pray for God's will in your relationships.
2. Try to agree with and/or come to consensus with those you know and love.
3. Think about what makes others in your life happy or get along with each other; try to help them to be in a state of harmony.
4. Evaluate your diet to ensure that your body is working harmoniously.
5. Host a party for close friends; enjoy each other's company.
6. Do what makes your significant other happy or content.
7. Peaceably converse with someone with whom you've had a disagreement.
8. Read your Bible asking God to show you something in his word to help you to live in harmony.

Girlfriend Patience

Prayer facilitated

toler**A**nce tested

posi**T**ive thinking

pra**I**se dependent

requir**E**s trust

forbeari**N**g

ne**C**essary

reward**E**d in time

Patience

Definition: bearing of provocation, annoyance or pain without complaint; ability to suppress restlessness or annoyance when delayed.

Origin: Middle English

Meaning: From the virtue

Bible Verses:

Habakkuk 2 v 3
For the vision is yet for an appointed time, but at the end it shall speak, and not lie: though it tarry, wait for it; because it will surely come, it will not tarry.

Romans 12 v 12
Rejoicing in hope; patient in tribulation; continuing instant in prayer;

Psalms 40 v 1
I waited patiently for the Lord; and he inclined unto me, and heard my cry.

Lamentations 3 v 25
The Lord is good unto them that wait for him, to the soul that seeketh him.

Isaiah 40 v 31
But they that wait upon the Lord shall renew their strength; they shall mount up with wings as eagles; they shall run, and not be weary; and they shall walk, and not faint.

Bible Reference:
1 Samuel 13 8-14

Saul's men were waiting for Samuel to arrive. After waiting seven days, they were becoming antsy and wanted to leave. To appease them, Saul offered up the burnt offerings. As soon as Saul had finished making the burnt offering, Samuel arrived. Samuel rebuked Saul for making the burnt offering and then proceeded to tell him what he forfeited by disobeying the command of God - which was having his kingdom established over Israel for all time.

Women of Patience in the Bible:

- *Elisabeth* - Though she was married for many years to Zacharias, they had no children. Elisabeth remained patient and waited on the Lord.
- *Hannah*, the favored wife of Elkanah could not bare children, suffered at the tongue of Elkanah's second wife and was after prayer and supplication granted grace and mercy in her son, Samuel. (1 Samuel 1; 2:1, 21)
- *Leah,* Jacob's first wife, bore him six sons which were to be six of the twelve tribes of Israel. Though despised by her younger sister, Jacob's second wife, she remained faithful to her husband and to God. The naming of her first four sons testified of this as their names mean; Behold a son, Hearing, Joined, and Praise. (Genesis 29; 30; 49:31; Ruth 4:11)
- *Manoah's wife and Samson's mother,* patiently waited on the Lord for him to end her barrenness and grant her a child. God appeared to both she and Manoah assuring them they would receive a very special son. Granted Samson, Manoah's wife became a joyous mother of a future judge of Israel. (Judges 13; 14:2-5; Hebrews 11:32)
- *Miriam,* the sister of Moses and Aaron, was obedient, patient and wise as she secured her mother to be Moses' nurse to the Pharaoh's daughter after placing him in the basket by the river; thereby saving his life. (Exodus 2 v 4)
- Saul's sons by Milcah and *Rizpah* (7 in all) were hung in revenge for Saul breaking an oath he'd made with the Gibeonites. All seven bodies were guarded by Rizpah for a long period of time to disallow the bodies to be ravished by natural scavengers until the rain came, after which the bodies were buried. (2 Samuel 3:7; 21:8-14)
- *Sarah* was 90 years old when she conceived a son to her long wedded husband, Abraham. Until God appeared to Abraham, they were childless. (Genesis 11:29-31; 12:5-17; 16:1-8; 17:15-21; 18; 20:2-18; 21:1-12; 23:1-19; 24:36, 37; 25:10, 12; 49:31)

About Patience:

Patience is specific as illustrated in our Bible verses and references above. Patience does not wait for *every*thing; she waits for a *specific* thing. Something that she has asked for, interceded for, prayed for, cared about, looked for, seen in her mind's eye or has been told by God that she will receive. She is specific in her posture of waiting, in her posture of prayer and in her posture of praise for what she knows will come as a reward of her patience.

Patience thinks positively and evokes feelings of positivity in those who wait. This is a tiresome job as many people, different to Patience, have not perfected praise in patience. They instead have perfected pouting, indifference, complaining, worry, weeping, self-pity, defeatism and some even surrender like Saul thereby forfeiting the reward.

Patience waits for you and seeks for you to perfect your praise in her. She seeks for you to, like Paul when segregated behind the prison walls of your circumstance, praise until the very walls fall down. She seeks for you to praise God in advance like Hannah did, as she waited for Him to bless her with a child to take away her shame. She seeks for you to, like the woman with the issue of blood, stand ready while waiting for the opportunity to touch the hem of His garment as He passes by. She seeks for you to labor and wait like Jacob for seven years for the hand of your desired spouse only to be tricked and made to labor without complaint for seven more years until your now past due reward is bestowed upon you. Patience seeks for you to perfect your praise while you wait.

Because of Patience:

I have yet to hear of anyone who has received the response from God to wait, that was not **prayerful.** Whether the prayers were full of bemoaning, whining, complaining or questioning is another thing altogether, but they prayed. Patience teaches us to to pray without ceasing. Patience forces us to surrender all to Him, for our prayers change when we encounter Patience. Instead of sappy, sympathy pleading prayers, Patience teaches us to surrender while we pray. Patience teaches us to pray The Serenity Prayer by Reinhold Niebuhr.

> God grant me the serenity
> to accept the things I cannot change;
> courage to change the things I can;
> and wisdom to know the difference.
> Living one day at a time;
> enjoying one moment at a time;
> accepting hardships as the pathway to peace;
> taking, as He did, this sinful world
> as it is, not as I would have it;
> trusting that He will make all things right
> if I surrender to His Will;
> that I may be reasonably happy in this life
> and supremely happy with Him
> forever in the next.   Amen.

As we are prayerful, we are also **persistent.** At the very least, we are persistent with our prayers, our petitions to our God. We are also persistent in hope and faith. We persist at being hopeful and faithful while we pray and yes, while we wait. We do not become weary in asking the Lord that He answer our prayers as He wills. This persistence, is not to force the hand of God, nor is the persistence always rewarded with the answer we seek; instead it is sometimes answered with a resounding, long-time in coming, NO, but whatever the answer may be; it is always for His will, to His glory and for our good.

Because we know that the reward for our patience is *always* for our good, while we wait, while we pray, and while we persist, we praise! Patience makes us **praiseful!** Though the only answer our Father has given us is to wait, we praise. We symbolically walk around the walls of our prayer request, just as the Israelite army walked around the reinforced, meant to endure, protective and defensive walls of Jericho. They didn't walk around timidly and coy. Instead they walked around with trumpets blaring, voices raised, and praise filled as they praised God before, to, through and after the faithful march. They praised, though they had no indication of when the walls would fall. They remained confident, steadfast, and resolved that the God who told them to, would show them how, reward their faith, their prayers, their persistence and their praise.

As a friend:

Patience is the least liked of the girlfriends. It is not that she does not have the dispositions of a good friend. It is that she always wants to wait, is not readily decisive or demanding and most of her girlfriends just don't like to wait. Her demand is two fold; that you wait and that you perfect your praise while you wait.

She is the girlfriend that is the last to make up her mind when deciding on the movie, the restaurant, the outfit she plans to wear, which car to buy, which neighborhood to live in, who to marry, etc. She insists that good things come to those who wait and tries incessantly to get everyone to wait for the good that will come into their lives. She encourages you, as you wait, to praise!

Patience, when passed over for the job she is due for, retreats to the essence of her virtue that she must wait and that in time, good will come to her. When faced with a delayed favorable response to a request for healing, Patience finds solace, dare I say happiness in the wait. For she knows that at the end of the wait; the answer, tailor-made and God-ordained for her, awaits.

Girlfriend to Girlfriend:
- Wait on the Lord.
- Though waiting is not easy, everything God has for you is well worth the wait.
- Perfect your praise while you wait.
- WAIT - You'll **W**in **A**ll **I**n **T**ime.

Patience in Quotation Marks:

"Waiting without whimpering, whining, wailing, weeping or worry."

Her Hashtags:
#waitingforthewin
#withoutworry
#praypraisewaitrepeat
#waitforHim
#perfecting praise

<u>Your Turn</u>

\# _____
\# _____
\# _____

Recognizing Patience:
- Pregnancy
- Waiting for healing without whining
- Waiting for a job without worry
- Waiting for a promotion without envy
- Completing a degree with determination through the years
- Praying a backslidden family member back to God
- Completing years of schooling
- Sitting on a plane on the tarmac without displeasure
- Sitting in a traffic jam without complaining
- Waiting for a paycheck when bills are due

<u>Your Turn</u>

- _____
- _____
- _____

Acknowledgement:
Waiting is such a hard thing to do! I must remember the story of Saul and Samuel. I have to be sure that whenever I think Patience and I simply must part ways that it is then that I must cling to her hand of friendship even more for however long an answer takes.

Reflection on Patience:
1. Your thoughts to or about Patience -

   _____
   _____
   _____
   _____
   _____

2. Romans 12 v. 12 introduces to us an unstoppable trio of girlfriends that we all should get to know. Which of the girlfriends in this verse do you need to get to know much better?

   _____
   _____
   _____
   _____
   _____

3. Hannah is often known to be a woman of patience; why might that be?

   _____
   _____
   _____
   _____
   _____

4. I have toyed with the idea of a personalized license plate reading, 'Patience' or 'W8', but I don't anticipate either of these plates stirring up any good feelings in the drivers behind me, so I've decided against it. Why might it be a good idea to take patience with you everywhere you go?

_____

_____

_____

_____

_____

5. Patience and another girlfriend are currently in an emotional struggle. Encourage them to remain friends with Patience...

_____

_____

_____

_____

6. There is little doubt that waiting is hard! Patience, on other hand, is never hard or difficult. What is the difference between waiting and exhibiting patience?

_____

_____

_____

_____

7. Complete an acrostic of the word, 'WAIT'. Share it on social media, see how many likes it gets.

_____

_____

_____

_____

8. Complete an acrostic of the word, 'PATIENCE'. Share it on social media, see how many likes it gets.

_____

_____

_____

_____

_____

Assignment:
1. Pray for the ability to be patient.
2. Show patience to someone to whom you've not been able to before.
3. Teach your children to be patient.
4. Patiently wait for your change to come.
5. Every time you open your mouth to complain, give praise instead.
6. Help someone pass the time while they wait; wait with them, talk to them; help take their mind off of whatever they are waiting for.
7. Pray with and for the other person or people you are waiting with.
8. Don't lose faith.
9. Read your Bible asking God to show you something in his word to renew your ability to be patient.

Girlfriend Prudence

Prepared

Resolute

Understanding

Discerning

Experienced

Neighborly

Connected to God

Economy-minded

Prudence

Definition: showing thought, care and action towards the future

Origin: Latin

Meaning: Cautious, Intelligent

Bible Verses:
Proverbs 19 v 14
House and riches [are] the inheritance of fathers: and a prudent wife [is] from the Lord.

Proverbs 15 v. 5
A fool despiseth his father's instruction: but he that regardeth reproof is prudent.

Proverbs 27 v 12
A prudent [man] forseeth the evil, [and] hideth himself; [but] the simple pass on, [and] are punished.

Bible Reference:
In the last verses of Luke 14, examples of prudence are shared by Jesus as he visited on the Sabbath day with one of the chief Pharisees. At the house, he met a man that suffered from dropsy. While others looked judgmentally to see if God would heal him on the Sabbath, Jesus proceeded to heal him and let him go.

At the end of the chapter, Jesus teaches about Prudence as follows:

Luke 14:28-32

28 For which of you, intending to build a tower, sitteth not down first, and counteth the cost, whether he have sufficient to finish it?

29 Lest haply, after he hath laid the foundation, and is not able to finish it, all that behold it begin to mock him,

30 Saying, This man began to build, and was not able to finish.

31 Or what king, going to make war against another king, sitteth not down first, and consulted whether he be able with ten thousand to meet him that cometh against him with twenty thousand?

32 Or else, while the other is yet a great way off, he sendeth an ambassage, and desireth conditions of peace.

Women of Prudence in the Bible:
- *Abigail* - Though miserable, Abigail remained married to her drunk, foolish, arrogant and ungodly husband. In wisdom she acted on behalf of her husband to expertly manage and conserve their affairs.
- *Anna* - A prophetess missionary through whom God used. She spoke of the coming of the Messiah.
- *Deborah (1)*- the nursemaid - She was Rebekah's nursemaid and lived a life of servitude as a faithful and loyal servant.
- Deborah *(2)*- a fearless patriot, wife, prophetess, agitator, ruler, warrior, poetess and maternal figure. She was a Proverbs 31 woman.
- *Jehosheba*, a princess married to high priest, courageously stole her nephew Joash to preserve his life and the royal seed of the line of Judah. (2 Kings 11:2; 2 Chronicles 22:11)
- *Joanna,* having being shown grace and mercy being healed from her infirmities, was numbered as one of Jesus' 12 and ministered to Jesus by giving of her plenty to meet his and his disciples' needs. (Luke 8 1-3)
- *Jochebed,* mother of Moses, devised a clever plan to have his life spared so that he could become one of the greatest leaders to the people of Israel in the Bible. Exodus 1; 2:1-11; 6:20; Numbers 26:59; Hebrews 11:23
- *Lois,* grandmother of Timothy won to Christ by the ministry of Paul. She, Timothy and Timothy's mother were stalwart believers in the Christ of whom Paul preached. (2 Timothy 1:5)
- *Lydia,* an astute business woman as she was well-known for her sale of purple dye. (Acts 16 v 14)
- *Martha,* was gracious and hospitable. She loved and served Jesus, her brother Lazarus and her sister Mary. (Luke 10:38-41; John 11; 12:1-3)
- *Mary,* the mother of Jesus, bore the prophetic child, Jesus, and cared for him providing him 'life', a home, moral lessons, mothering as one would a soon coming King. (Luke 1:28, 30)
- *Ruth,* daugher in law to a widowed and aging Naomi, sought work in order to provide for herself and Naomi upon their return to Jerusalem. (The Book of Ruth)

- *Wise Hearted women*, served the church by joyfully, willingly and without reward hand making woven cloths for the completion of the Tabernacle of the Lord. (Exodus 35 vs 22-29)

About Prudence:

Prudence is busy, concerned and consumed with the things that matter to those she loves, cares for, and meets. She incessantly considers shelter, raiment, provision, finances. She plans, and analyzes what is needed, what will come next, who should be involved; what should happen; when something should occur; where it will take place, why and how. Prudence is prudent and therefore leaves no stone unturned.

Prudence is not afraid of or daunted by correction. Instead, she sees it to be a way to improve herself, to do better the next time and have things have a better result than they had before. Prudence is not at all occupied with self-pity nor is ruffled by reproof providing it is done with tact, taste, empathy and love; as that is the manner by which she provides instruction or correction.

Prudence thinks about us with a goal of having us to despise folly, not be made to look like fools, to encourage us to first, think, plan and then act upon a well-devised plan. Prudence because of her well-calculated thought patterns as well as her gift of foresight is able to avert discomfort or disasters by avoiding them. Prudence has a high level of common sense, which others say she uses for the betterment of all.

The foresight that Prudence has is not self-achieved; it is granted by God to Prudence as she listens intently and gives due diligence to what the Lord has to say to her. She acts in accordance with His will, is careful to first seek His voice then move only as he directs.

Prudence feels that her attributes as modeled can be emulated as others can see the worth of what she does, the potential benefit to their own lives and those with whom they are entrusted. Others say that Prudence can be counted on to be there for you, is a planner, is a model woman and is future-focused.

Because of Prudence:

A sense of prudence compels you to be **prepared.** This heightened need to be prepared impacts everything; your plans, your finances, your children, your job, your career, your family, even where you will spend eternity; everything. You have the need to leave nothing to chance. You feel you must prepare amply for everything. Preparation for a woman of Prudence is active, because she must physically and/or spiritually put things in order if you are to avoid the opposite of preparation which is undeniably, panic. Prudence seeks to avoid panic, even though the avoidance of panic is time consuming and invasive. Prudence and preparation go hand in hand.

In order to be prepared, you have to be **planned**. It is simple, without a plan, you fail. Prudence despises and avoids failure like the plague it is. She carefully articulates a plan for how things are to work in the best case scenario, then works diligently following each step of the plan with precision to ensure that the plan is successful. Because of Prudence's very nature, you will have a big picture idea of where you are going, what you want to accomplish and how you intend to get there. The plan could be in your thoughts, scribbled on paper, or recorded painstakingly detail by detail, but for certain, because of Prudence you have a plan that takes into consideration those who may affect your plan, financial constraints, ideological roadblocks and various other potential barriers to your success with plans A, B and even C detailing how you can circumvent them.

Because of Prudence you are are intentionally **purposeful.** You know your purpose and if you don't as yet, you trust God without reservation or hesitation to have you live and work in your purpose even though you may not know specifically what it is. You believe that the purpose for which God has purposed you is part of His divine plan. You believe that He knows the plans He has for you and that if He reveals His plan for your life to you; it's okay and you will obey. If He does not, it is still okay and you still will obey.

It is quite uncanny, but whether you know His plan for your life or not, you, because of Prudence wake every day to fulfill your purpose. This is only possible because of a surrendered dependence on God and a realization that despite your best efforts, you cannot, will not, nor could not influence or defer from your purpose. You are predestined, there is a plan for your life and you are purposed and your very existence is purposeful.

As a friend:

Prudence is the girlfriend that everyone seems most comfortable using as a sounding board. She is the friend that is going to listen to you intently, weigh each word, analyze the tone of the conversation, interpret your body language, judge your commitment, ask you clarifying questions, insist that you write your thoughts down, look at it from a different angle, consider the alternatives, evaluate the consequences of the decision, think about 'what if this, then this...' scenarios, and then expect that you are able to make a decision, summarize the conversation, and then pen a follow-up date to the conversation on her calendar, all in one sitting.

Prudence is also the friend that insists that you make some preparation for your future; personally, educationally, financially, spiritually. She is going to put ever before you the question of 'what next?' She may empathize with you regarding perceived failures be they personal or professional but she will not spend any time wallowing in self-pity or prolonged indecision. She will take you through the steps outlined above with an efficiency that will either frustrate or motivate you; either way… to action.

Prudence is a financially astute friend. She is going to weigh every decision through both a common sense and a financial lens. She wants you to wear her lenses when decisions are made as well. She is the friend that on every 'shopping' trip fills her cart, bag or forearm with clothes, tries each piece on, and whether they fit or not; leave the store with either empty arms or with bags filled significantly less than yours. She is therefore typically, the friend with the most money saved, providing she is independent financially, as she is always thinking about and planning for an inevitable rainy day.

Prudence is a planner, she is the friend that probably married later in life than all of the rest of you. She may be the friend that has one or more degrees, has the business plan that is sure to be profitable, and/or is a power broker in her current employ.

If married, Prudence is the wife every husband should want for her care of her home, family, spouse and children is her priority and she deals with each prudently. For this reason, Prudence may be discounted by her girlfriends as being one with whom they can spend time, enjoy life or hang out with. She is sometimes viewed as standoffish, stuck-up and/or a prude. Girl talk is different around Prudence; not that it should be, but the other girlfriends just aren't sure about what they can discuss with Prudence, just how far the conversation should go. Almost all of the girlfriends, with the exception of Honesty and maybe Joy, are too cautious to 'take the chance' for fear of offending Prudence.

Girlfriend to Girlfriend:
- Remember to balance self-sufficiency and your need for others.
- Be sure that you take time for yourself, as you plan and prepare for everyone and everything else.
- Trust your senses.
- Think before you plan, plan before you act, then act and never give up.

Prudence in Quotation Marks:

"Concern and diligence to, preparation for and fidelity toward all of concern."

Her Hashtags:
#futurefocused
#decisionmaker
#commonsenseprue

#preparedprue
#jobdone

<u>Your Turn</u>

\# _____

\# _____

\# _____

Recognizing Prudence:
- Contentment
- Future Planning
- Seeking degrees
- The humble housewife
- Getting the job done

<u>Your Turn</u>
- _____
- _____
- _____

Acknowledgement:
With all that I am afforded and have been blessed with; grant me the discernment to act according to the benefit it will afford someone else. Help me not to be wasteful or ungrateful regarding the intellect and resources that I have been granted. Help me to recognize Prudence in myself and my girlfriends, and to follow her example to honor home, family, spouses and our God in all that we do and say.

Reflection on Prudence:
1. Your thoughts to or about Prudence -

   _____

   _____

   _____

   _____

2. Which of the women noted above, is your favorite woman of prudence? Why?

   _____

3. Prudence has a partnership with planning, preparation, prayer, and reflection. Put them in order and explain how they are related to each other.

_____

_____

_____

_____

_____

4. Which of your girlfriends is the 'Prue'? Which characteristics does she have most in common with Prudence? Which do you most appreciate? Which do you wish you possessed?

_____

_____

_____

_____

_____

Assignment:
1. Pray for God's will regarding everything in your life.
2. Do something special for your neighbor or the elderly.
3. Offer assistance to a child struggling with a school subject.
4. Complete your degree.
5. Carefully manage your finances.
6. Pray about and make plans to better your life.
7. Honor your commitments in your marriage and other relationships.
8. Give to those in need.
9. Read your Bible asking God to grant you wisdom regarding the matters of your life.
10. Claim and live the promise of Jeremiah 29 v 11.

Girlfriend Justice

Just

trUth

Satisfying

righTeous

Impartial

Complete

Equitable

Justice

Definition: being fair and reasonable

Origin: French

Meaning: Justice

Bible Verses:
Hosea 12 v 6
Therefore turn thou to thy God: keep mercy and judgment and wait on thy God continually.

Micah 6 v 8
He hath shewed thee, O man, what is good; and what doth the Lord require of thee, but to do justly, and to love mercy, and to walk humbly with thy God?

Zechariah 7 v 9
Thus speaketh the Lord of hosts, saying, Execute true judgment, and shew mercy and compassions every man to his brother:

Psalm 106 v 3
Blessed are they that keep judgment, and he that doeth righteousness at all times.

Bible Reference:
Though Justice is the third sibling of Grace and Mercy in Genesis 3, I presented her to you from another book of the Bible.

1 Kings 3

One of my favorite Bible stories is about Justice as it also speaks strongly of a mother's love. Outside of its theme, the story is quite disturbing as it tells of two mothers who were sleeping with their young children beside them. One of them inadvertently rolled over and smothered her child to death. She, after realizing what she did, rose from where she slept, went to the bed of the other woman, switched the children and returned to her bed with the other woman's child.

When King Solomon heard the case, he made the decision to cut the surviving child in half as both of the women claimed the baby was hers. As this decision was simply unthinkable to the mother of the child; she insisted that they allow her to surrender the child to the other woman rather than have her child to die. King Solomon, in wisdom, delivered justice by restoring the child to his mother.

Women of Justice in the Bible:
- *Deborah* - a prophetess and a judge - she had the gift of discernment, was spoken to and through by God. She dispensed judgments of grace and mercy sitting under a tree bearing her name. She was also a warrior and gained fame by defeating her enemies and rescuing her people.
- *Mahlah, Noah, Hoglah, Milcah and Tirzah* - became precedent setters by standing up and claiming possession of their father's (Zelophehad's) inheritance.
- *Huldah* was consulted when the lost book of the law was found. Huldah's prophetic message and the reading of the law brought about a revival in the land.
- *Puah and Shiprah,* two Egyptian midwives who were in charge of a large number of midwives were directed to kill the Israelite males upon their births. The women together determined that true to their faith they could not do such and claimed that the babies were born they could get to them, thereby sparing their lives. (Exodus 15 v. 1-21).
- *Rahab,* hid the men of God, and provided them a way to avoid sure death while placing herself on the treason punishable road herself. Instead of punishment, she was offered grace as God spared she and her family from Jericho's impending doom. (Joshua 2:1, 3; 6:17-25)
- *Wench of En-Rogel,* thwarted Absalom's plan against his father by covering an empty well thereby hiding David's men. She also sent them in a direction away from David's men they pursued. (2 Samuel 17:17-19)
- *Wise woman of Abel,* delivered up Sheba who was an accepted traitor. Sheba was beheaded and the city of Abel was saved. (2 Samuel 20:16-22)
- *Woman of Tekoah,* convinced David to bring Absalom, banished for killing Ammon, back home and eventually face justice. (2 Samuel 14:1-20)
- *Woman of Thebez*, single handedly except for God slung a rock onto King Abimelech's neck leading to his death in recompense for him killing off all those who may have been in line to be king (69 brothers). Abimelech in his last few moments of consciousness begged his armor bearer to kill him lest it be said he was killed by a woman. (Judges 9:50-57; 2 Samuel 11:21)

About Justice:

Justice, though she carries the responsibility of and for justice, balances this responsibility with fairness. Justice tempers her decisions with mercy for we do not have the capacity to handle what we deserve. Her feelings toward us are tempered with grace and mercy. She is not blinded by grace and/or mercy but instead filters her just will through them.

Many seek and praise Justice. They actively seek her as they want her to intervene on their behalves when wronged and to vindicate them when accused or blamed. They actively praise her because they recognize her role in their lives as they benefit from her intervention.

She is incapable of being unfair, though at times her decisions may have you feel that she is being so. She aims to maintain a well-orchestrated equilibrium that honors justice, rewards fairness, spreads hope and optimism, consequences evil and renews our faith in God's Divine Plan.

Others recognize that Justice is necessary, especially in this increasingly perverse and wicked world. She restores our hope that evil and wrong are going to be punished and that right and good is preferred, sought after and valued. She encourages us to pursue her even though she may be elusive, difficult to find, or may not bring our desired result. Many highly regard Justice as she is kind, giving, forgiving, restorative, and just.

Because of Justice:

A **judicious** state of mind is a constant for Justice. You too, because of Justice, are also incapable of nonsense, folly, or poor judgment. It is difficult to near impossible for you to switch justice off, because you are wired to seek right, the truth and judgment. You are able to enjoy life, appreciate humor and to see the lighter side of things, but you cannot stomach when humor unfairly tips the balance between right and wrong. You cringe at the very thought of someone's self-image, self-esteem and/or feelings of self-worth being compromised due to an injustice dealt to them. This judicious state of mind compels you to deal fairly with everyone, to honestly and fairly interact with others and to seek to mercifully right wrongs done to others.

Because of Justice and Mercy, you are **justified**. Being justified, you are declared or made righteous in the sight of God. You are not perfect, but justified. You are not a saint, but justified. You enjoy the privilege of having been declared righteous in God's sight. Regardless of your life's experience, you are fully aware that this justification is only as a result of God's grace and mercy tempered justice to you, for He did not deal with you as you rightfully deserved. He tempered His justice with His grace and mercy and rendered you righteous in His sight. If that does not make you feel special, I don't know what will. You are righteous, justified, in His sight, the Almighty's sight, the omniscient God who knows you and everything about you, what you did last night, who you were with, what you took from the job today, how late you got to work, who you lied to, what you lied about, what your very thoughts are, and still He looked at you through the eyes of Justice through the lenses of Grace and Mercy and declared you justified.

As a friend:

Justice is very matter of fact, she is honest, clear with her speech, decisive and draws the line in the sand every chance she gets.

Justice, Honesty and Mercy hang out together at all times. If you were to see one of these ladies, the other is close by as they complement each other well. They can finish each other's sentences as they are always thinking about what is truth. Ensuring that things that are just, true, lenient and fair are what gets their attention.

As a friend to all, Justice is caring, compassionate, merciful, patient, and humble. Justice gains no pleasure in dispensing deserved consequences to those with whom she interacts. She instead offers an empathetic ear, shares the reasons for the consequence and behooves the 'consequenced' to improve their behavior; to go and sin no more.

Justice is the friend you want with you when you are called to the boss' office, the director's trailer, or the courthouse. She will hold your hand, remind you to brace for the verdict and trust that regardless of what is shared as you sit with pensive breath, that she is righteous, true and fair.

Girlfriend to Girlfriend:
- Deal fairly with everyone you meet.
- Be thankful that Mercy and I are friends.
- A deeper knowledge of me is what the world desperately needs.
- Pattern yourself after me, I seek to improve you, not only deliver justice.

Justice in Quotation Marks:

"Receiving what is deserved tempered with grace and mercy."

"Receiving what is deserved restrained by grace and mercy."

Her Hashtags:
#fairandtrue
#allthatisjust
#mercifulandfair

#justreward
#justfair

<u>Your Turn</u>

\# _____
\# _____
\# _____

Recognizing Justice:
- Every just decision
- A fair verdict
- An opportunity for a another chance
- A blessing

<u>Your Turn</u>

- _____
- _____
- _____

Acknowledgement:
    Please help me to be fair and reasonable with everyone I meet. Help me to temper my thoughts, choices, my decisions and my actions with Justice. Help me to embrace Justice when her judgement appears not to be fair to me, or is in contrary to my desires. Help me to recognize that Justice is truth, righteous and required by God.

Reflection on Justice:
1. Your thoughts to or about Justice -

_____
_____
_____
_____
_____

2. King Solomon was a king of Justice. In the story referenced about the two mothers, what was he also a king of?

_____
_____
_____
_____
_____

3. Often we entangle Justice with the idea that she should also bring favor, positivity, contentment, or satisfaction. Is it possible for there to be Justice and there still be discontentment or dissatisfaction?

_____
_____
_____
_____
_____

4. Express your feelings concerning Justice, Mercy and Grace being siblings.

_____
_____
_____
_____
_____

5. The last woman introduced as a woman of Justice; the Woman of Thebez, single-handedly delivered justice to King Abimelech. What does this suggest about the strength of Justice?

_____
_____
_____
_____
_____

6. The world needs love, undeniably! Make the case that our world also needs Justice.

_____
_____
_____
_____
_____
_____
_____
_____

Assignment:
1. Pray for God's justice to touch everything that concerns you.
2. Read the Bible to discover and learn more about our God of justice.
3. Temper justice dealt to your children with mercy.
4. Reason with those who are unreasonable.
5. Be fair with everyone.

Girlfriend Joy

Jubilation
Overflows
alwaYs

Joy

Definition: feeling of great pleasure or happiness; delight

Origin: French

Meaning: Joy

Bible Verses:
Philippians 4 v 4
Rejoice in the Lord always. Again I will say, rejoice!

Psalm 118 v 24
This *is* the day the Lord has made;
We will rejoice and be glad in it.

Psalm 16 v. 11
You will show me the path of life;
In Your presence *is* fullness of joy;
At Your right hand *are* pleasures forevermore.

Nehemiah 8:10
Then he said unto them, Go your way, eat the fat, and drink the sweet, and send portions unto them for whom nothing is prepared: for this day is holy unto our Lord: neither be ye sorry; for the joy of the Lord is your strength.

Psalm 30:5
For his anger endureth but a moment; in his favour is life: weeping may endure for a night, but joy cometh in the morning.

Bible Reference:
Philippians

Paul was a prisoner being punished for spreading the gospel of Christ. Yet, he wrote the "Book of Joy" - Philippians. He was serving prison time, restrained, shackled, confined and unhappy, yet he encouraged those in the prison and those who would read his books to press on, to rejoice always and to press toward the mark of the high calling of Jesus Christ.

Women of Joy in the Bible:
- *Joanna,* having being shown grace and mercy after she was healed from her infirmities, was numbered as one of Jesus' 12 and ministered to Jesus by giving of her plenty to meet his and his disciples' needs. Her joy came from service and allegiance to her master even unto his death. She heralded the fact that he was no longer dead but risen after His aromatic burial. (Luke 24:1-12).
- *Leah*, Jacob's first wife, bore him six sons which were to be six of the twelve tribes of Israel. Though despised by her younger sister, Jacob's second wife, she remained faithful to her husband and to God. The naming of her first four sons testified of this as their names mean; Behold a son, Hearing, Joined, and Praise. (Genesis 29; 30; 49:31; Ruth 4:11)
- *Manoah's wife and Samson's mother,* patiently waited on the Lord for him to end her barrenness and grant her a child. God appeared to both she and Manoah assuring them they would receive a very special son. Granted Samson, Manoah's wife became a joyous mother of a future judge of Israel. (Judges 13; 14:2-5; Hebrews 11:32)
- *Martha and Mary* after the raising of their brother, Lazarus from the dead. (Luke 10:38-41; John 11; 12:1-3)
- *Mary,* the mother of Jesus, experienced and uttered pure joy as well as her belief in Messianic prophecy in Luke 1:46-55.
- *Sarah* was 90 years old when she conceived a son to her long wedded husband, Abraham. Until God appeared to Abraham, they were childless. Isaac's birth made Sarah a woman of joy. (Genesis 17 and 18)
- *Susana,* healed both physically and spiritually by God, became a woman of joy, followed and served Jesus and his disciples out of her provision. (Luke 8:2, 3)
- *Wise Hearted women*, served the church by joyfully, willingly and without reward handmade woven cloths for the completion of the Tabernacle of the Lord. (Exodus 35 vs 22-29)
- *Woman of Shunem,* In return for her hospitality, she received the promise of and later a son, making her a woman of joy for the first time. The son died and Elisha at the request of his grief stricken mother restored him to life, making her a woman of joy for the second time. (2 Kings 4:8-37; 8:1-6)

About Joy:
    Joy goes beyond smiling, being happy or elated. Joy experiences an internal contentment, satisfaction, hope, vibrancy and fulfillment that resembles that of her friend Serenity; being difficult to explain but a joy to experience.

    Her feelings toward you are of the same; a desire to have you to experience contentment; despite the imbalances in various areas of your life. She desires for you to be satisfied with what you have; who you are with; where you work; with whom and where you worship; how much money there is or is not in your bank account. She desires for you to have hope that confounds those who know about your circumstances; that your spouse abuses you, that you are unemployed, that you've just received notice of foreclosure and the car you were driving home just died on the side of the road leaving you stranded. She desires for you to bounce out of bed every morning, though today may end up being just like yesterday with little to eat, no affirmative answer about the job prospects and the car being due to be repossessed.

    She desires for you to experience the fulfillment that only Christ gives, as He looks at all that is broken, disjointed, destructive, destroyed, painful, bankrupt in your life yet He chooses to allow you to borrow his breath to fuel your being, whisper in your ear to have you wake up, have the sun to shine on your face and allow you to feel and see it, give you food and raiment, and stretch the dollars you receive though underpaid. Joy allows you to experience fulfillment because God is not surprised nor was caught off guard by your current circumstance. He seeks to provide for you what gives you your joy. He seeks to determine if you will allow all He has chosen to give you to be smothered by the weeds of self-pity, ingratitude, and all that seeks to shackle Joy. He seeks to determine if you know where Joy comes from, who grants it and who cannot take it away.

    As Joy's feelings are those that breathe life, energy, positivity and hope into every situation; her actions evidence her feelings. Joy busies herself spreading her sentiment to everyone. She looks for those that are downtrodden, hopeless, depressed, unhappy and surrendered and gently nudges them into a posture of reflection on the goodness of the Lord, followed by a posture of praise brought on by honest introspective reflection. As praise is infectious, freeing, revealing, and extrospective, Joy compels you to a joyous state which is the result of purposeful praise.

Because of Joy:
    Joy makes you **joyful,** full of joy. It is impossible to witness someone full of joy that does not exude it; make it appealing; inviting and contagious. When we have joy we are able to smile at any circumstance; we are able to skip and run though crippled and expected to walk; we are able to show to others the joy of the Lord even when

circumstances appear daunting and impassable. Joy gives you hope which turns into faith and trust. Joy allows you to be strong in the strength of the Lord regardless of the opposition and your personal failings. Joy bolsters you, supports you and has you to forever have praise on our lips, declaring from the mountaintop or the valley, that joy, pure, unadulterated, God-given joy will come in the morning.

You are **just** because of joy. Psalm 119 v. 1-3 says it better than I ever could;

1 Joyful are people of integrity,

who follow the instructions of the Lord.

2 Joyful are those who obey his laws

and search for him with all their hearts.

3 They do not compromise with evil,

and they walk only in his paths.

So, while those who deal unjustly are flaunting their success, their wealth, social position or societal ranking, those that have the joy of the Lord are wealthier, better off and destined for heaven as they walk in integrity, follow God's instructions, obey His laws, search for Him, are uncompromising with evil and as a result walk only in His paths. Speak about a treasure laid up for women of Joy in heaven! Joy allows you to be just and be joyous here on this temporal Earth in order to without regret enjoy an eternal home in heaven.

Joy in tribulation is afforded when you have joy.

James 1:2-4

2 My brethren, count it all joy when ye fall into divers temptations,

3 knowing this: that the trying of your faith worketh patience.

4 But let patience have her perfect work, that ye may be perfect and entire, lacking nothing.

We can have joy in tribulation, because it builds our faith, it builds our spiritual stamina. Joy builds our faith, and by the building of our faith, we perfect our praise through patience. Patience's work is perfect and complete as accurately recorded in the Bible, so it would behoove us to let her work, and at the end there is nothing that we will need, or not have! That enduring promise allows me to have JOY while still in the tribulation!

As a friend:

Joy possesses something indescribable. She is not giddy or silly; neither is she bashful or shy. Instead, she is bold, friendly, happy, content, pleasant and satisfied.

She exudes confidence, contentment, delight, and exuberance. She does things that gives her immense pleasure; things like service, giving, sharing, teaching, and forging friendships. She looks for the very best in everyone she meets, and is ecstatic when she finds joy within others.

Joy is infectious. Once she steps into the room, she circulates the room quickly and infectiously. Before she is introduced, Joy is recognized by the beaming smile she greets everyone with. Upon introduction, Joy creates an atmosphere that is pleasant and consumingly agreeable. Those with whom she interacts can't help but get drawn into the highly positive conversation with which she engages. Joy is the life of the party, but not in a self-gratifying manner. She simply desires to draw others into her aura of joy.

Joy encourages you to see the silver lining of every cloud of life, though it may be all but invisible. She is not affected by a snub by others, getting cut-off in traffic or receiving bad news. She simply makes the adjustment, confident that there is a reason for everything that happens in her life and though she may not know the reasons, God does. As a friend she impresses on you daily to believe as she believes, trust as she does and rejoice in the Lord always and again. She implores you to rejoice!

Joy reminds you of the best in life. She reminds you that every day is a day the Lord himself has granted you and that you should and have been commanded to be glad in it. She spends no time with self-pity or worry; she lives every day committed to the promise that she is God's and that He has begun a good work in her and is faithful and just to see it until the joyful end.

Girlfriend to Girlfriend:

- Never let anyone quiet your praise!
- Choose joy!

Joy in Quotation Marks:

"Strength in the struggle while waiting for the morning."

Her Hashtags:

#joyful
#fulfilledandhappy
#can'thaveit
#Godgivenstrength
#rejoicealways

Your Turn

\# _____
\# _____
\# _____

Recognizing Joy:
- Contentment
- Praise
- Giving thanks
- Smiling, regardless of the situation
- Encouraging others, despite your current circumstances

Your Turn
- _____
- _____
- _____

Acknowledgement:

    I want the joy that Joy has. I want the confidence that she walks around with. I want the joy of the assurance that God knows and will show me the path I should take in life. I want the satisfaction that oozes from Joy. She is never distracted, worried, or discontent. She always has joy. Grant me this joy and neither let me surrender it, nor take it for granted.

Reflection on Joy:

1. Your thoughts to or about Joy -

   _____
   _____
   _____
   _____
   _____

2. Why is Joy equated to strength?

   _____
   _____
   _____
   _____
   _____

3. Joy demands that you rejoice always, and recognize that each day is a day the Lord made in which we should be glad. How is it possible to be joyous always?

   _____
   _____
   _____
   _____

4. Many of the women of Joy became women of Joy when they became mothers. If you can relate, how is that the same for you?

   _____
   _____
   _____

_____

_____

5. Can you have Joy without gratitude? Why or why not?

_____

_____

_____

_____

_____

Complete the equation:

Joy - Gratitude = _____

6. Can you have Joy without praise? Why or why not?

_____

_____

_____

_____

_____

Complete the equation:

Joy - Praise = _____

7. Is it true that joy cannot be stolen? How do you know?

_____

_____

_____

Assignment:
1. Thank God for the joy he has given to you.
2. Smile.
3. Share a kind word with someone.
4. Laugh.
5. Encourage or motivate someone.
6. Watch a comedy.
7. Do what makes you happy.
8. Do something good for someone else.
9. Reflect on and ponder the goodness of our God.
10. Spend time with your children, family and the love ones in your life.

Girlfriend Glory

God's

Love given to

Our fallen race to

Restore us to Him

Yet, without sin.

1 Peter 5 v 10 (ESV)
And after you have suffered a little while, the God of all grace, who has called you to his eternal glory in Christ, will himself restore, confirm, strengthen, and establish you.

Glory

Definition: great beauty; cause for pride; honor, worship, praise or valor

Origin: Latin

Meaning: worship, praise or valor

Bible Verses:
Psalms 3 v 3
But thou, O LORD, [art] a shield for me; my glory, and the lifter up of mine head.

Proverbs 19 v 11
11 The discretion of a man deferreth his anger; and it is His glory to pass over a transgression.

1 Corinthians 10 v 31
Whether therefore ye eat, or drink, or whatsoever ye do, do all to the glory of God.

Bible Reference:

Genesis 45

Joseph had been sold by his brothers as a reward for their jealousy and Jacob's favoritism shown toward him. Joseph was consequently taken to Egypt to be a slave. Joseph, over time, was rewarded for his loyalty and service by being promoted to being in charge of the land.

As the land had years of plenty and were now in a time of famine as Joseph interpreted Pharaoh's dreams to announce; Joseph's family had to go to Egypt to find grain. The brothers had no idea that Joseph was living such a blessed and glorious life in Egypt. Upon a subsequent visit to purchase grain, Joseph could no longer keep from them that he was their brother. He shared with them that it was for God's glory that he was sent to Egypt to be lord of Pharaoh's house. He gave them lots of gifts, food and provision so that they could return to their father and country. He also encouraged them to tell his father about his glory earned, garnered and afforded to him in Egypt. Joseph had a glorious ascent from the hole to honor.

Women of Glory in the Bible:
- *Abia or Abiah* - knew and honored God as her Heavenly Father.
- *Dorcas* - earned fame and prestige for her dress-making. She was also an avid philanthropist and she gave away everything she had and could to those in need to the honor and glory of God.
- *Huldah* was consulted when the lost book of the law was found. Huldah's prophetic message and the reading of the law brought about a revival in the land. (2 Kings 22:14-20; 2 Chronicles 34:22-33)
- *Jecholiah,* wife to a king and mother of a king, sought God and to God's glory, her son did right in the sight of the Lord as king. (2 Kings 15:2; 2 Chronicles 26:3)
- *Jehosheba*, a princess married to high priest, courageously stole her nephew Joash, hid him for six years to preserve his life and the royal seed of the line of Judah. (2 Kings 11:2; 2 Chronicles 22:11)
- *Joanna,* having being shown grace and mercy, being healed from her infirmities, was numbered as one of Jesus' 12 and ministered to Jesus by giving of her plenty to meet his and his disciples' needs. Her joy and glory came from service and allegiance to her master even unto His death. She heralded the fact that He was no longer dead but risen after His aromatic burial. She was one of the last women to see Jesus at his burial and one of the first to proclaim He was risen. (Luke 24:1-12).
- *Jochebed,* mother of Moses, devised a clever plan to have his life spared so that he could become one of the greatest leaders to the people of Israel in the Bible. Exodus 1; 2:1-11; 6:20; Numbers 26:59; Hebrews 11:23
- *Leah,* Jacob's first wife, bore him six sons which were to be six of the twelve tribes of Israel. Though despised by her younger sister, Jacob's second wife she remained faithful to her husband and to God. The naming of her first four sons testified of this as their names mean; Behold a son, Hearing, Joined, and Praise. (Genesis 29; 30; 49:31; Ruth 4:11)
- *Lois,* grandmother of Timothy, won to Christ by the ministry of Paul. She, Timothy and Timothy's mother were stalwart believers in the Christ of whom Paul preached. (2 Timothy 1:5)

About Glory:

Glory is our anticipated and expectant end. God has promised in Colossians 3 v 4 that *When Christ, who is our life, shall appear, then shall ye also appear with him in glory.* This is our blessed hope. Glory then has thoughts and feelings toward you to draw you closer to Christ. She spends her time telling you about what it would be like to be with Jesus forever. She paints a vivid, appealing and reverential picture of what it would be like to be able to serve forever with Jesus. She spends time thinking about the glory of heaven and never ceases to inspire you to join her there.

Glory is a dreamer, but not in a negative connotation of the word. She is a dreamer, she hopes, she believes in a sure promise that is echoed numerous times in scripture that her heavenly father is coming back to summon us to glory. She is also a planner, because she so firmly believes the promises of God, she orders her life accordingly. She obeys the ten commandments, morally aligns with all of the virtues and expectantly awaits his return.

Glory's heart is burdened for you, she is burdened for your rising up and your going down, she is burdened regarding your daily comings and goings, your hopes and dreams, your pain and sorrow, your today and tomorrow. She is burdened for you for she knows that as life presses down mercilessly on you at times, it is at times appealing to give in to the sins that will so easily beset us, take us off course, change our direction, change our mission and purpose, and consequently change our destination. Glory therefore stays on her knees interceding on our behalves for she has her eyes fixed on the desire of each and every one of our hearts, and works tirelessly to have us to likewise remain transfixed on the glory of heaven.

She spends all her time, seeking the lost, encouraging the downtrodden, inspiring those who need inspiration, reminding all of God's love and his glory, insisting that everyone treat others as they would like to be treated; remain joyful in tribulation, wait on the Lord, leniently and honestly deal with and relate to others, honor their responsibilities, seek peace and pursue it, hope in the Lord, walk daily by faith, claim God's favor, understand that the benefits of grace and mercy are free, unmerited and should be shared, and to love everyone with an everlasting love.

Because of Glory:

Because of the promise of glory, we are **guarded.** Under his wing, we are perfected, confirmed, strengthened and established as stated in 1 Peter 5 v. 10.

> After you have suffered for a little while, the God of all grace,
> who called you to His eternal glory in Christ, will Himself perfect,
> confirm, strengthen and establish you.

God, in order to ensure that eternal glory is attained by us, protects us though we suffer for a little while. His word plainly says that we may suffer now but it won't always be a life of suffering. We will be able to perfected and strengthened while in the midst of the struggle and when we come out of our dark valley, we will go on to our eternal glory.

The promise of Glory also makes us **grateful**. We remain grateful, for the one and only God who is glorious, deserves our honor and our praise. He chose to suffer and die by the hands of a cruel, insidious people with a painful crown of thorns on his head so that we live blissfully, rapturously forever with Him. That singular act, if God were to do *nothing else* for us must render us forever grateful.

This gratitude is best demonstrated, by being **God-fearing.** No, we are not afraid of God, we fear or reverence, we honor, and we praise him. We fear Him and Him alone because from Him we get our very breath, we have command of our limbs, because of Him, we are. Without Him, we would cease to be. We can do nothing without Him, we are compelled to reverence Him, submit to His will, follow His commandments, read His word, remain in constant communication with Him through prayer, cast all of our cares upon Him, trust Him ONLY with our heart, our soul, our life, our love. We fear and worship God because He deserves it, and because He created us to do so. We fear God all the way to Glory!

As a friend:
Glory is who each girlfriend strives to be like. They don't envy her, for they know that her substance and her worth has been gifted yet earned, awarded yet aspired toward, benevolent, yet not free. Glory has put in the time in prayer, worship, adoration, reverence, and labor to receive her reward. Glory is the friend that shows you by example to how you should live, how you should relate to others, how you should love and who you must believe. She does not spend much time lecturing you, she simply lives before you in as an impeccable example of virtue.

Glory reads and believes the Bible, so her conversations with you are always centered around the word of God and getting to heaven. She does not 'glory' in anything that is not of the Lord. Whereas she loves her family undeniably, cares about her career and lifestyle, takes classes to better herself, and even may have a hobby that pays or helps others, she takes no glory in any of that. For her, glory is reserved for the things of God, period! Glory is her only goal. She encourages you to aspire greatness in all the superlatives of life as she does; but relentlessly reminds you that this world is not our home and we are simply passing through!

For this reason, she insists that you, like her, not put your hand to do anything that God has not told, inspired, instructed, or commanded you to do. She knows that time doing anything contrary to God's plan is futile, worthless, and a waste of the temporary time that you have here on earth. In every conversation, she asks the question, 'Is this for Christ or is it for you?' Glory befriends you so that you can deny yourself on this Earth and make plans to be certain to see her revealed in the Earth Made New.

Girlfriend to Girlfriend:

- Be grateful for and hold dear to all that is gifted to and precious to you.
- Remember to pray and give thanks for all that you've been blessed with.
- Deny yourself here so that you can get over there!
- Heaven's glory is your goal.

Glory in Quotation Marks:

"High praise and honor earned, bestowed upon or offered to one as deserved."

"The rapturous temporal ending and the celestial eternal beginning."

Her Hashtags:

#deserveddelight
#allpraisetoGod
#holyhonor
#crownedinvalor
#forgiveforhonor
#virtueclad
#heavenfocused
#heavenbound

<u>Your Turn</u>

_____
_____
_____

Recognizing Glory:
- Nature
- Gifts of God
- Praise
- Worship
- Forgiveness
- Contentment
- God
- Honor

- Salvation
- Heaven

Your Turn

- _____
- _____
- _____

Acknowledgement:

Like Joseph, help me to chose my own glory through the act of forgiveness to those who seek to or do offend me. Help me to know that it is my glory to claim. Help me to live my life in accordance to Your will and plan of salvation for me granted to my forefathers in the Garden of Eden. Help me to trust the plans you designed for my life and to dedicate my life daily to honor and glorify only You! Help me to stay true to the purpose of my creation which is to worship you. Equip me to remain focused on my heavenly home.   Amen.

Reflection on Glory:

1. Your thoughts to or about Glory -

   _____
   _____
   _____
   _____
   _____

2. Relate your reaction to Colossians 3 v 4 *When Christ, who is our life, shall appear, then shall ye also appear with him in glory.*

   _____
   _____
   _____
   _____
   _____

3. Who offers you glory (in the defined sense of the word) and for what is the glory offered?

_____
_____
_____
_____

4. Think of your last three life decisions. Evaluate whether they were the decisions made for you or for Christ?

_____
_____
_____
_____

5. A woman's long hair in 1 Corinthians 11 v 15 is noted to be her glory. Is this to be literally interpreted? Why or why not?

_____
_____
_____
_____

6. In Isaiah 60 NIV, The Glory of Zion is eloquently and comprehensively explained. As I read it I likened the city of Zion to my life/experience. I read it as if it were written for me, a woman; I could feel hope, faith, trust, favor, peace, joy, redemption and glory all wrapped up in the written word. Read it; do you have the same experience?

_____
_____
_____

7. Why is Glory listed as the last of the girlfriends from the Bible?

_____

_____

_____

_____

_____

Assignment:
1. Tell someone about Christ.
2. Live every day in preparation for Glory.
3. Celebrate someone else's accomplishments.
4. Celebrate your own accomplishments.
5. Encourage someone today.
6. Remind others of the happiness, joy, peace, and harmony gained in Christ.
7. Prepare and hope for the day when Christ returns.

Girlfriend You

Each girlfriend that befriends you in their uniqueness, is highly cognizant and aware that you are a unique girlfriend too. They recognize and appreciate all that you are, all that you bring to the table, all that you give to the friendship, all that your friendship affords them. They can see each of their characteristics in you and in each other. They are able to assist you in cultivating their unique attributes in yourself all with the intent to help you chart your path to Glory.

These girlfriends have grown with you, though they were all born at Creation, they continue to refine you through their age old wisdom, and their uncanny ability to see you like no one else quite can. They continue to draw out of you the best in you and the best in those around you by their immersive presence, their contagious influence and their undying devotion and loyalty to you.

Regardless of how you define yourself in the next few pages, they have a picture of you that is more pristine, more transparent, more reflective of you than you can ever see yourself as, for they have accompanied you when times are bad, when life is tough, when joy is abundant, when peace has escaped you, when disappointment overwhelms you, when you are on the brink of giving up and will be with you when you receive your promised victory. They know you when it is difficult for you to recognize yourself, for you weren't supposed to be his doormat, you weren't supposed to be his ATM, you weren't supposed to be his whore. You weren't supposed to drop out of school, you weren't supposed to be pregnant the first time, nor this time, you weren't supposed to alienate yourself from your family and all of your girlfriends.

You were supposed to be phenomenal, fearless, fierce, and fabulous. Trust me, by strengthening the friendship with each girlfriend you've just learned about, you will be. For God has fashioned each of the girlfriends, each of the fourteen introduced to you in the pages prior and the one destined to write the next chapter in this book and in her own life. God did not create you or I to be failures or to be forgotten but since the beginning of time He fashioned us in the fear of himself. That leaves me in awe.

The next chapter is about you, yes, for you are one of the girlfriends. So, write your chapter, learn about your name, define it, find out its origin, and its meaning. Dictate the Bible verses and references that most resonate with you. Write about yourself, about you as a friend, about how you can be recognized, quote yourself, and create a hashtag or two about you. Identify women in the Bible you most regard or resemble and then make your acknowledgement about yourself public, let God know that you are His and only His. Let God know that you know that all that you are, can be, and will be is because of Him.

fearfullY and

wOnderfully made,

yoU

Your Name _____

Definition:

_____

Origin:

_____

Meaning:

_____

Bible Verses that most resonate with you and your life's experiences:

_____
_____
_____
_____
_____
_____
_____
_____

Bible Reference that you most identify with based on your life experiences and resultant praise:

About You:

Because of You:

You as a friend:

_____
_____
_____
_____
_____
_____
_____
_____

You in Quotation Marks:

"_____"

Your Hashtags:

                                      #
                                      #
                                      #
                                      #
                                      #

Recognizing You:

-
-
-
-
-
-

Acknowledgement:

_____
_____
_____

_____
_____
_____
_____
_____

Women in the Bible you most regard or resemble. Who are they and why?

- _____
_____
_____
_____

- _____
_____
_____
_____

- _____
_____
_____

Proverbial Portraits of The Girlfriends

The Girlfriends as described in the book of Proverbs follow. Heralded to be a wise king, Solomon proliferated bigamy as outlined in 1 Kings 11 v. 3. He had seven hundred wives, princesses, and three hundred concubines: and his wives turned away his heart. Bathsheba, his mother, after her forgiveness by God, is believed to pen this letter in Proverbs 31 to Solomon, and all other men, though clearly he and so many others did not heed it.

Those men that have heeded Bathsheba's counsel have often gone on to forget the worth of a virtuous woman once wed by taking her for granted, discarding her or abusing her for evidences of her virtues. Others, honor her virtue and live happy, harmonious lives together forever.

Though not every girlfriend is seeking to be or are married; every girlfriend can identify with the virtuous woman described in Proverbs as they vividly and candidly evidence the highly desirable attributes described from the tip of Queen Bathsheba's pen. May we all aspire to be women of virtue.

As described, Honesty is the underpinnings for the other virtuous women; so the honest question posed in verse 10 requires a frank answer and a vivid portrait of what a virtuous woman looks like, is, demonstrates, illustrates, lives, and embodies as captured in the following verses by each of the other girlfriends to complete the well-crafted, fearfully and wonderfully made woman.

Proverbs 31 v 10 - 31 and *The Girls* mirrored

Honesty

10 Who can find a virtuous woman? for her price is far above rubies.

Harmony and Serenity

11 The heart of her husband doth safely trust in her,

so that he shall have no need of spoil.

Grace and Mercy

12 She will do him good and not evil all the days of her life.

Patience

13 She seeketh wool, and flax, and worketh willingly with her hands.

Hope

14 She is like the merchants' ships; she bringeth her food from afar.

Grace and Mercy

15 She riseth also while it is yet night, and giveth meat to her household, and a portion to her maidens.

Prudence

16 She considereth a field, and buyeth it: with the fruit of her hands she planted a vineyard.

Joy

17 She girdeth her loins with strength, and strengtheneth her arms.

Faith

18 She perceived that her merchandise is good: her candle goeth not out by night.

Harmony

19 She layeth her hands to the spindle, and her hands hold the distaff.

Charity

20 She stretcheth out her hand to the poor; yea, she reacheth forth her hands to the needy.

Serenity

21 She is not afraid of the snow for her household: for all her household are clothed with scarlet.

Favor

22 She maketh herself coverings of tapestry; her clothing is silk and purple.

Favor

23 Her husband is known in the gates, when he sitteth among the elders of the land.

Prudence

24 She maketh fine linen, and selleth it; and delivereth girdles unto the merchant.

Honesty and Joy

25 Strength and honour are her clothing; and she shall rejoice in time to come.

Justice

26 She openeth her mouth with wisdom; and in her tongue is the law of kindness.

Hope and Justice

27 She looketh well to the ways of her household, and eateth not the bread of idleness.

Glory

28 Her children arise up, and call her blessed; her husband also, and he praiseth her.

Charity

29 Many daughters have done virtuously, but thou excellest them all.

Faith

30 Favour is deceitful, and beauty is vain: but a woman that feareth the Lord, she shall be praised.

Patience and Glory

31 Give her of the fruit of her hands; and let her own works praise her in the gates.

Which Girlfriend Are You Most Like?

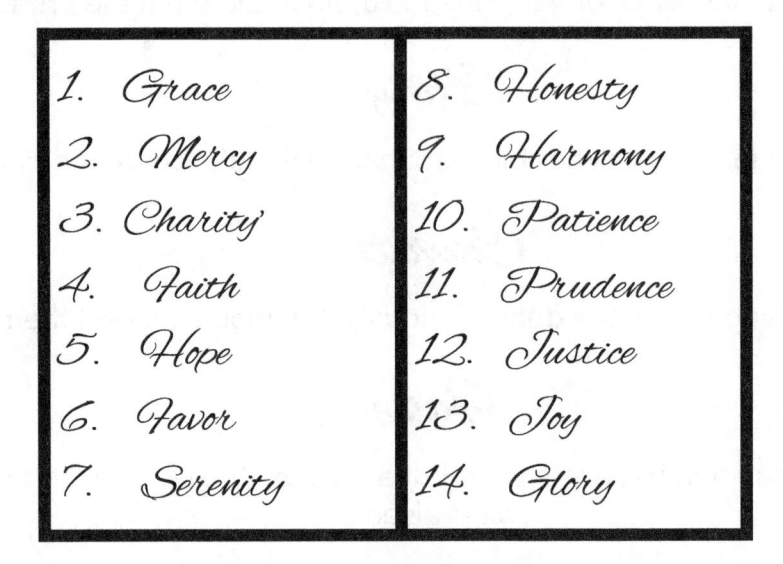

1. Grace	8. Honesty
2. Mercy	9. Harmony
3. Charity	10. Patience
4. Faith	11. Prudence
5. Hope	12. Justice
6. Favor	13. Joy
7. Serenity	14. Glory

Make a list of the three Girlfriends you believe you are most like.

1. _____

2. _____

3. _____

Then take the assessment to determine which girlfriend's dispositions best describe you.

Circle only 12 dispositions that <u>best</u> describes you in the grid below (Be selective!)

1. I am true and truth.
2. I prefer not to get what I deserve.
3. I show kindness to those who don't deserve it.
4. I am neighborly to all I meet.
5. I love unconditionally.
6. I deal fairly with others.
7. I avoid conflicts.
8. I let God fight my battles.
9. I believe that I will be victorious in any situation.
10. I give praise when it is due.
11. I possess an inner contentment about life.

12. I praise when it's difficult to do so.
13. I am always thinking and looking ahead.
14. I get along with almost everyone I know.
15. I have inner strength that others can readily see.
16. I pray and don't worry.
17. I like to give gifts.
18. I pray.
19. I have a highly contagious personality.
20. I am thoughtful and well-planned.
21. I tell the truth regardless of the cost.
22. I think positively regardless if the circumstance.
23. I don't see time as a barrier.
24. I go to bat for those who don't deserve it.
25. I use my power to empower others.
26. I don't see obstacles, barriers or limits.
27. I get along with most everyone.
28. I am an optimist.
29. I am loyal.
30. I have many people indebted to me.
31. I look for opportunities to and bless others.
32. I have a high honor system and moral code.
33. I am honorable.
34. I do not have favorites.
35. I insist that we look on the bright side of things.
36. I am even-keeled regardless of the situation.
37. I am straightforward.
38. I prefer to let my walk, talk.
39. I prefer to see others improve rather than be punished.
40. I am in a consistent state of mental calm.
41. I get along with most everyone.
42. I am sensitive and lenient.
43. I see people as unique and necessary.
44. I am married.
45. I am beautiful.
46. I am a communicative mediator.
47. I am praise worthy.
48. I am single.
49. I am a woman.
50. I am intuitive and instinctive.

Identify your choices to the questions as grouped below. The girlfriend(s) with the most responses are who you are most like!

Which *Girlfriend* are you most like?
Virtue Finder

Grace	*Mercy*	*Charity*	*Faith*	*Hope*
Questions 5, 17, 24, 29	Questions 2, 3, 31, 42	Questions 5, 19, 25, 29	Questions 9, 18, 26, 38	Questions 18, 22, 26, 28
Total:	Total:	Total:	Total:	Total:
Favor	*Serenity*	*Honesty*	*Harmony*	*Patience*
Questions 3, 17, 29, 31	Questions 7, 27, 36, 40	Questions 6, 21, 34, 37	Questions 14, 43, 46, 50	Questions 12, 16, 22, 23
Total:	Total:	Total:	Total:	Total:
Prudence	*Justice*	*Joy*	*Glory*	*You Are:*
Questions 4, 13, 20, 32	Questions 1, 6, 8, 39	Questions 11, 12, 15, 19	Questions 10, 33, 45, 47	1. 2. 3.
Total:	Total:	Total:	Total:	

149

The Parting Sentiment of Each Girlfriend's Heart

                                                          Monthly/Daily/Always

Dear Girlfriend,

        Those things, which ye have both

              learned, and received,

          and heard, and seen in me,

                      do:

and the God of peace shall be with you.

                Philippians 4 v 9

                                                        Yours,
                                                          The Girlfriends

References

Bible Gateway - https://www.biblegateway.com/

Holy Bible - King James Version - Public Domain.

The Serenity Prayer - Reinhold Niebuhr (1959).